Country Living

Pies&Tarts

· COUNTRY BAKER ·

Pies&Tarts

THE EDITORS OF
COUNTRY LIVING MAGAZINE

Foreword by Rachel Newman

Country Living

HEARST BOOKS · NEW YORK

Photography Credits
Pages 17, 54, Jerry Simpson
Pages 18, 71, Irwin Horowitz
Page 35, Dennis M. Gottlieb
Page 36, Victor Scocozza
Pages 53, 72, Richard Jeffery

•

•

It is the policy of William Morrow and Company, Inc., and its imprints and affiliates,
recognizing the importance of preserving what has been written, to print the books we
publish on acid-free paper, and we exert our best efforts to that end.

•

Library of Congress Cataloging-in-Publication Data
Country Living.
Country living, country baker. Pies & tarts : foreword by
Rachel Newman. — 1st ed.
p. cm.
Includes index.
ISBN 0-688-12543-3 (alk. paper)
1. Pies. I. Country living (New York, N.Y.)
II. Title. III. Title: Country baker. IV. Title: Pies & tarts. V. Title: Pies and tarts.
TX733.C6345   1993
641.8'652—dc20
92-33222
CIP

•

Printed in Singapore
First Edition
1 2 3 4 5 6 7 8 9 10

•

Country Living Staff
Rachel Newman, *Editor-in-Chief*
Lucy Wing, *Contributing Food Editor*
Joanne Lamb Hayes, *Food Editor*
Elaine Van Dyne, *Associate Food Editor*

Produced by Smallwood and Stewart, Inc., New York City

Edited by Judith Blahnik
Designed by Tom Starace
Cover designed by Lynn Pieroni Fowler

Contents

....

Foreword

....

What is more evocative of the delights of home than the vision and aroma of fresh-baked pies set out to cool on the sill? For this reason Thanksgivings at my house have always been the ultimate test of will power. No matter how grand the main feast may be, everyone's real goal is to save some room so they can have, in the words of my aunt, "just a little sliver of each." It's no surprise that somehow these sample pieces never allow a pie to fall into the category of leftovers.

Because the editors at *Country Living* are so aware of America's continuing love affair with pies, we frequently use them as props when photographing our country kitchens. But we've learned a lesson about these "prop" pies — if they look too good, with the juices oozing over the sides of the tins, we'd better include a recipe for them. If we don't, we're bound to get hundreds of letters requesting one!

Whether you crave the hearty meat filling of a shepherd's pie or the more refined sweetness of a tart, this collection of recipes is sure to satisfy your every taste.

Rachel Newman
Editor-in-Chief

Introduction

....

Americans love eating pie so much that we have blessed it with the
patriotic "as American as apple pie" slogan and given it its own
holiday, National Pie Day — January 23rd.

One reason we like pie is because it doesn't demand a special occa-
sion in order to come to the table. Taking a fork to a golden flaky
crust wrapped around sweet summer peaches, or sliding into a shim-
mering lemon meringue, or spooning up a warm, sweet-crusted cherry
cobbler are traditional endings to a home-cooked meal any day, every
day if we like. We pursue good pie, often waiting to be seated in tiny
overcrowded restaurants where homemade apple, peanut butter, cherry
crumb, and sweet potato pies are made fresh daily. We find ourselves
in bakeries, oohing and aahing over beautiful glazed fruit and nut
tarts. And one of our favorite comfort meals is a light chicken stew
baked in a delicate crust.

As much as we love pies, however, we seem to have a phobia about
making them. Turning out a tough, unfriendly crust seems to be our
number one fear. After all, a beautiful lattice-crust has got to be as light
and tender as it looks. Here is a collection of some of our favorite sweet
and savory American classic pies with a no-fault pastry recipe and tips
to help you turn out a delicious pie fearlessly.

About The Ingredients

Our recipes require unsifted all-purpose flour unless otherwise
noted. For some biscuit pastry we use fresh double-acting baking

powder. Check the date on the can to make sure yours is fresh. If you have any doubt, stir 1 teaspoon into ½ cup hot water. If there's a bubbling reaction, the baking powder is fresh.

Fresh fruits are washed and berries are picked over and rinsed. Butter is lightly salted and always in the stick, as is margarine if you choose to use it. Don't substitute whipped butter, liquid or tub spread margarine. They contain more water and less fat than stick, and while they may be better for you on the dinner table, they do not make for better pastry dough. Don't substitute vegetable shortening with vegetable oil, and use the type of sugar suggested in the recipe.

The cocoa powder we use in our chocolate crusts and cream fillings is unsweetened, and when we call for chocolate squares, they are the 1-ounce squares found in bakers' chocolate. Eggs are always large and stored in their cartons in the refrigerator. Don't substitute any ingredients unless noted in the recipe.

We recommend that you try to use real rather than imitation vanilla, maple, and almond extracts. The pungent flavor of the authentic extract adds character to your pie or tart. Spices such as cinnamon, allspice, ginger, and cloves should be checked for freshness. If your jar or can is more than six months old, the spice may deliver disappointing results. Nutmeg is always best when freshly grated from the whole nutmeg. When we call for walnuts, almonds, pecans, and hazelnuts (filberts), it's in their natural unblanched state unless otherwise noted.

Some of our recipes call for liqueurs, which add flavor and fragrance to certain traditional pies. In most cases, you can substitute a fruit juice for a liqueur.

About The Equipment

Give yourself a space 26 by 26 inches to roll out the pastry dough with a sturdy rolling pin. Three different-size mixing bowls and a set of metal dry measuring cups and glass liquid measuring cups are essential. A pastry blender is a tool that cuts rather than blends fat into flour, and a pastry brush is handy for applying glaze.

Bake the pie or tart in the plate or tart pan size suggested in the recipe, measuring the distance between the inside edges of the rim. We prefer glass pie plates because they are sturdy, they conduct heat evenly, and they allow you to see how the pastry is browning. Metal pie tins are fine to use, but thin aluminium are often too flimsy to adequately support a pie. Use standard 9- and 10-inch tart pans with removable bottoms and 3½-inch and 4-inch tart pans.

An assortment of cookie cutters can turn pastry scraps into decorative finishing touches on the top crust or border of the pie. For adding scalloped cream borders and meringue lattice tops, we use a pastry bag with assorted tips; washable nylon and disposable plastic both work well.

A wire or wooden cooling rack is necessary because pies and tarts must cool evenly on a surface that allows air to circulate. Buy a rack large enough to cool at least two pies or tarts.

About The Method

For the purposes of saving space, we haven't described certain techniques in detail. When the recipe says "cool on a wire rack," it means to cool the pie or tart to room temperature. When the recipe directs you to "remove the side of the pan," as in our tart recipes, it means to place the bottom of tart pan on a wide-mouth jar and gently slip the removable side down.

Berry-Cherry Pie

....

This is a refreshing and imaginative mix of berries with sweet and sour cherries. You choose from your favorites — boysenberries, blue-berries, gooseberries, and huckleberries are all delicious when combined with cherries.

MAKES ONE 9-INCH PIE

Pastry for a Two-Crust Pie (page 83)

Berry-Cherry Filling:
6 cups assorted fresh berries and pitted sweet and sour cherries

¾ cup sugar
⅓ cup all-purpose flour or 3 tablespoons cornstarch
2 tablespoons lemon juice
½ teaspoon grated lemon rind
2 tablespoons butter, melted

1. Prepare the pastry and on a lightly floured surface, roll out half to an 11-inch round. Fit into a 9-inch pie plate, leaving the edge untrimmed.

2. Prepare the Berry-Cherry Filling: Heat the oven to 400°F. In a large bowl, combine the berries and cherries, all but 1 teaspoon of the sugar, the flour, lemon juice, lemon rind, and butter. Spoon the berry filling into the pastry-lined plate. Top with a lattice crust, page 27. Sprinkle the reserved sugar over the pastry strips. Place the pie on a rimmed baking sheet.

3. Bake 40 to 50 minutes, or until the filling bubbles in the center. Cool on a wire rack.

....

CHOOSING YOUR CHERRY

The Bing is a widely available sweet cherry. When ripe, it is a deep red color and firm to the touch but not hard. The Early Richmond sour cherry variety is a bright red and less firm than the Bing but not soft. Cherries are in season June through August. Buy the ones with stems attached; they last longer than the batches without stems.

....

Deep-Dish Plum Pie

....

Once a characteristic American summertime dessert, plum pie is seldom seen nowadays. We suspect it's because of the time it takes to pit and quarter the plums. We encourage you to take the time. This is a delicious treat that should be declared a national treasure. Select greengage or purple plums that are uniform in color and slightly soft to the touch.

MAKES ONE 12- BY 8-INCH PIE

Pastry for a One-Crust Pie
(page 82)

Plum Filling:
¾ cup sugar
½ cup all-purpose flour
2 pounds firm red or purple
plums, quartered and pitted
1 pound greengage plums or
prune plums, quartered
and pitted

1 tablespoon orange juice
1 teaspoon grated orange rind
2 tablespoons butter or
margarine, cut into small
pieces

Vanilla ice cream or frozen
yogurt (optional)

1. Prepare the Pastry for a One-Crust Pie. On lightly floured surface, roll out the pastry into a 13- by 9-inch oval for a 12- by 8-inch oval baking dish 2½ to 3-inches deep.

2. Prepare the Plum Filling: Heat the oven to 425°F. In a large bowl, combine the sugar and flour until well mixed. Fold in the plums, orange juice, and orange rind. Spoon the plum mixture into the baking dish; dot with butter. Place the pastry over the filling. Fold the edge of the pastry just under the inside rim of the dish; press the pastry to the rim of the dish. Cut slits in the crust to allow steam to escape during baking.

3. Bake the pie 55 minutes, or until the filling bubbles in the center. Cool on a wire rack. Serve with vanilla ice cream, if desired.

Fresh Strawberry Pie

....

Strawberries are available all summer long and in some parts of the country all year, but we find the sweetest and most flavorful ones at the grocers during May, June, and early July. Buy berries with an unmistakable strawberry fragrance. This perfume is the best indicator of sweet, ripe quality. Also, look for good color and make sure the leafy green hulls are attached.

MAKES ONE 9-INCH PIE

Baked 9-inch Piecrust
  (page 82)

Strawberry Filling:
2 tablespoons cornstarch
1 cup granulated sugar
1 cup water

1 3-ounce package strawberry-
  flavored gelatin
2 pint baskets (4 cups)
  strawberries

Sweetened Whipped Cream:
1 cup (½ pint) heavy cream
1 tablespoon confectioners' sugar

1. Prepare the Baked 9-inch Piecrust.

2. Prepare the Strawberry Filling: In a 2-quart saucepan, combine the cornstarch and granulated sugar; slowly stir in the water until blended. Cook over medium heat, stirring constantly, until thickened and bubbly. Add the gelatin, and stir until it dissolves. Remove from the heat. Cool the gelatin mixture to room temperature but do not allow it to get cold, or it will be too firm to pour over the strawberries.

3. Meanwhile, rinse and hull the strawberries. Drain well on paper towels. Spread the strawberries evenly in the piecrust. Pour the thickened gelatin mixture over the strawberries. Cover and refrigerate the pie 2 to 3 hours, or until the gelatin is set.

4. Prepare the Sweetened Whipped Cream: Just before serving, in a small bowl, with an electric mixer on medium speed, beat the cream and confectioners' sugar until stiff peaks form. Spread the whipped cream over the top of the pie. Serve immediately or refrigerate until ready to serve.

Peach Pie

To peel a peach, plunge it into rolling boiling water for 30 seconds and then into very cold water. The skin will slip off easily.

MAKES ONE 10-INCH PIE

*Pastry for a Two-Crust Pie
    (page 83)*

Peach Filling:
*3 pounds peaches, peeled,
    pitted, and sliced, or
    6 cups thawed, drained,
    frozen peach slices*
2 tablespoon lemon juice

½ teaspoon almond extract
½ cup sugar
⅓ cup cornstarch
½ teaspoon ground nutmeg
¼ teaspoon salt
*1 tablespoon butter or
    margarine, melted*
1 teaspoon sugar (optional)

1. Prepare the Pastry for a Two-Crust Pie.

2. Prepare the Peach Filling: In a large bowl, toss the peaches, lemon juice, and almond extract. In a small bowl, combine the sugar, cornstarch, nutmeg, and salt. Add the sugar mixture to the peaches, and toss until well combined.

3. Heat the oven to 400°F. On lightly floured surface, roll out half the pastry into a 12-inch round. Fit the pastry into a 10-inch pie plate, leaving the edge untrimmed. Pack the peach mixture firmly into the pastry-lined plate.

4. Roll out the remaining pastry into a 10-inch round. With a fluted pastry wheel or sharp knife, cut the round into twelve ¾-inch-wide strips. Twist the strips and place crisscross over the top of the filling, pressing the ends into the edge of the pastry. Fold the edge under so that it is even with the rim of the plate; flute pastry edge. Brush the pastry strips with butter. If desired, sprinkle 1 teaspoon sugar over the top of the pie.

5. Bake the pie 55 minutes, or until the filling bubbles in the center. Remove the pie to a wire rack. While the pie is still hot, brush some bubbling juice from the edge of the pie onto the peaches in the center. Cool on the rack.

Strawberry-Port Pies

....

E ven though these are fun-to-make little pies, each wrapped in an old-fashioned all-in-one crust, the taste of ruby port and the pleated top crust make them slightly more elegant than everyday. To make one pie instead, use a 9-inch pie plate and roll out all the pastry into one 16-inch round.

MAKES FOUR 4-INCH PIES

Pastry for a Two-Crust Pie
   (page 83)

Strawberry-Port Filling:
½ cup sugar
¼ cup cornstarch

1 cup ruby port
2 pint baskets (4 cups)
   strawberries, rinsed,
   hulled, and halved
1 tablespoon butter or
   margarine, melted

1. Prepare the Pastry for a Two-Crust Pie.

2. Prepare the Strawberry-Port Filling: In a 1-quart saucepan, combine the sugar and cornstarch. With a wire whisk, gradually whisk the port into the sugar mixture. Heat the mixture to boiling over medium-high heat, stirring constantly; remove from the heat.

3. Heat the oven to 400°F. Divide each half of the pastry into 2 pieces. On lightly floured surface, roll out each piece of into an 8-inch round. Using an 8-inch round baking pan as a guide, trim the edge of each pastry round with a fluted pastry wheel or sharp knife. Fit each pastry round into a 4-inch tart pan, leaving the edges untrimmed.

4. Fold the strawberries into the port mixture. Divide the mixture among the pastry-lined pans. Lift the excess pastry over the filling, leaving a hole in the center. Pleat the pastry where necessary to fit tightly over the filling. Brush the pastry with the butter.

5. Bake the pies 40 minutes, or until the filling bubbles in the center. Cool on wire racks.

Rhubarb Custard Pie

A thicker, creamy custard-style pie, we call this the city cousin to our country Rhubarb Pie, page 19.

MAKES ONE 9-INCH PIE

Unbaked 9-inch Piecrust
(page 82)

Rhubarb Custard Filling:
1 pound rhubarb, without
tops, trimmed, rinsed, and
cut into ¼-inch slices

¾ cup sugar
¼ cup all-purpose flour
3 eggs
½ cup sour cream
1 teaspoon vanilla extract

1. Prepare the Unbaked 9-inch Piecrust.

2. Prepare the Rhubarb Custard Filling: Heat the oven to 350°F. In a large bowl, combine the rhubarb, ½ cup sugar, and the flour. Spoon the rhubarb mixture into the piecrust.

3. In a small bowl, lightly beat the eggs. Stir the sour cream, the remaining ¼ cup sugar, and the vanilla into the eggs. Spoon the mixture over the rhubarb mixture.

4. Bake the pie 45 to 50 minutes, or until the filling bubbles in the center. Cool on a wire rack.

BRINGING HOME THE RHUBARB

Buying rhubarb is not a tricky outing. Look for firm, crisp celery-like stalks, either pink or cherry red in color. If the grocer hasn't removed the leaves, do so just before baking. They are inedibly toxic. Fresh is best. Buy it no more than one day before baking and keep it cool or it will wilt. Rhubarb is very tart. In the Middle East, it is cooked with almost no sweetener and served as a piquant accompaniment for meats. Here and in England, we love to combine rhubarb with sugar and sometimes other fruits in any number of filled pastry desserts.

Pears in Port on Cornmeal Shortbread Crust, page 58

Rhubarb Pie, page 19

Rhubarb Pie
PHOTOGRAPH ON PAGE 18

R hubarb was once called "pie plant" because it grew well in any gar-
den and was inexpensive, easy pickings for baking. It is still in abundance April to June and certain hothouse varieties are available year
round. Buy it fresh and use it within three days, as it is highly perishable.

MAKES ONE 9-INCH PIE

*Pastry for a Two-Crust Pie
(page 83)*

*Rhubarb Filling:
2 pounds rhubarb without
tops, trimmed, rinsed, and
cut into 1-inch pieces*

*1½ cups sugar
⅓ cup all-purpose flour
1 teaspoon grated lemon rind*

1. Prepare the Pastry for a Two-Crust Pie.

2. Prepare the Rhubarb Filling: In a large bowl, combine the
rhubarb, sugar, flour, and lemon rind; let stand at least 15 minutes.

3. Heat the oven to 400°F. On a lightly floured surface, roll out half
the pastry into an 11-inch round and fit into a 9-inch pie plate, leaving
the edges untrimmed. Pour the filling into the pastry-lined plate. Top
with lattice crust, page 27.

4. On a lightly floured surface, roll out the pastry trimmings into
1½-inch-wide strips. Cut the strips diagonally into 2-inch-long pieces.
With water, moisten the bottoms of the pieces. Arrange the pieces,
overlapping, around the rim of the pie plate.

5. Bake the pie 50 to 60 minutes, or until the filling bubbles in the
center. Cool on a wire rack.

DAY-AHEAD DOUGH

O ur basic pastry doughs can be made ahead, wrapped and refrigerated up to 3 days. The extended chilling doesn't hurt the dough.
In fact it relaxes the gluten and helps the flour absorb moisture. Allow
long-chilled dough to sit out 10 minutes or so before rolling.

Blueberry Cheese Pie

....

This is a beautiful marriage of berries and creamy cheese in a crisp graham cracker crust topped with sour cream. We warn against any substitutions here. These ingredients bring out the best in each other. If your only encounter with blueberries has been bland out-of-hand eating, try this pie for a whole new experience!

MAKES ONE 9-INCH PIE

Graham-Cracker Crust
  (page 85)

Blueberry Cheese Filling:
2 8-ounce packages light
  cream cheese, softened
½ cup sugar
2 tablespoons all-purpose flour
2 eggs
2 teaspoons vanilla extract

½ cup half-and-half
1 pint basket (2 cups)
  blueberries
1 teaspoon grated lemon rind

Sour Cream Topping:
1 8-ounce container light
  sour cream
2 tablespoons sugar

1. Prepare the Graham-Cracker Crust: Make the crust ahead, but do not bake it.

2. Prepare the Blueberry Cheese Filling: Heat the oven to 350° F. In a food processor fitted with the chopping blade, process the cream cheese and sugar until smooth. With the processor running, add the flour, eggs, vanilla, and half-and-half through the feed tube; process until smooth. Turn the food processor off and add 1 cup blueberries and the lemon rind to the cheese mixture; process by pulsing just until half the blueberries are chopped. Pour the blueberry mixture into the crust-lined plate.

3. Bake the pie 35 minutes. Meanwhile, prepare the Sour Cream Topping: In a small bowl, combine the sour cream and sugar. Spread the sour cream topping over the blueberry cheese layer, and bake the pie 10 minutes longer, or 45 minutes total. Cool the pie completely on a wire rack. Refrigerate the pie at least 8 hours or overnight. Just before serving, garnish the pie with the remaining 1 cup blueberries.

Streusel Peach Pie

....

One of the best things you can do with a fresh summer peach (besides eat it right off the tree) is to bake it simply in this open-face pie.

MAKES ONE 9-INCH PIE

Butter Pastry:
2¼ cups all-purpose flour
½ teaspoon salt
1 cup (2 sticks) butter or
    margarine
3 to 5 tablespoons cold water

Peach Filling:
8 medium-size peaches,
    peeled, halved, and pitted
¾ cup granulated sugar
1 teaspoon grated lemon rind
1 tablespoon lemon juice
½ cup firmly packed
    light-brown sugar

1. Prepare the Butter Pastry: In a medium-size bowl, combine 2 cups flour and the salt. With a pastry blender or 2 knives, cut ¾ cup butter into the flour until the mixture resembles coarse crumbs. In a small bowl, reserve 1 cup of the flour mixture for the streusel topping.

2. Stir the cold water, one tablespoon at a time, into the remaining 1 cup butter-flour mixture, and mix lightly until the pastry holds together when lightly pressed. Shape the pastry into a ball. Wrap and refrigerate at least 30 minutes. On a lightly floured surface, roll out the ball into an 11-inch round. Fit the pastry into a 9-inch pie plate. Fold the pastry overhang under so that it is even with the rim of the pie plate and flute the edge.

3. Heat the oven to 400°F. Prepare the Peach Filling: Cut the peaches into thick slices. In a large bowl, toss the peaches, granulated sugar, lemon rind, lemon juice, and the remaining ¼ cup flour. Spoon the filling into the pastry-lined plate.

4. Stir the brown sugar and remaining ¼ cup butter into the reserved butter-flour mixture until crumbly. Sprinkle evenly over the peaches.

5. Bake the pie 40 minutes. Cover the top of the pie with a circle of aluminum foil and bake 20 minutes longer, or until the filling bubbles in the center. Cool on a wire rack.

Red, White, and Blue Pie
PHOTOGRAPH ON PAGE 72

It's the fresh blueberries, raspberries, and whipped-cream topping that give this pie its patriotic look and make it the perfect ending to a 4th of July celebration. A caveat: If you do take this pie to an Independence Day picnic, be sure to keep it well chilled until ready to serve.

MAKES ONE 11-INCH PIE

Sweet Pastry:
2¼ cups all-purpose flour
⅓ cup sugar
½ teaspoon salt
¾ cup vegetable shortening
1 teaspoon vanilla extract
4 to 6 tablespoons ice water
1 egg
1 tablespoon milk

Berry Filling:
2 cups raspberry-cranberry
*   juice drink*

5 tablespoons cornstarch
¼ cup sugar
3 pint baskets (6 cups)
*   blueberries*
1 teaspoon vanilla extract
2 tablespoons orange-flavored
*   liqueur*
4 half-pint baskets (4 cups)
*   raspberries*

½ cup Sweetened Whipped
*   Cream (page 13)*

1. Prepare the Sweet Pastry: In a medium-size bowl, combine the flour, sugar, and salt. With a pastry blender or 2 knives, cut the shortening into the flour mixture until the mixture resembles coarse crumbs. Stir in the vanilla and 4 tablespoons ice water, one tablespoon at a time, just until the mixture holds together when lightly pressed. Add more ice water, if necessary. Shape the pastry into a ball; flatten to a 1-inch thickness. Wrap and refrigerate at least 30 minutes.

2. Heat the oven to 400°F. On a lightly floured surface, roll out the pastry into a 14-inch round. Fit the pastry into an 11-inch pie plate. Trim the pastry even with the rim of the pie plate. With a fork, pierce the bottom and side of the pastry. If desired, roll the pastry scraps to a ¼-inch thickness and, with a sharp knife or a 2-inch star shaped cookie cutter, cut out as many 1- to 2-inch stars as possible. With water, moisten the stars and press them around the edge of the pie, spacing evenly, to form a border.

3. Line the piecrust with aluminum foil and add uncooked dried beans or pie weights. Bake the piecrust 10 minutes. Meanwhile, in a small bowl, beat the egg and milk. Remove the beans and foil from the piecrust and brush the crust with the egg mixture. Bake the piecrust 10 to 12 minutes longer, or until golden. Cool the piecrust completely in the pan on a wire rack.

4. Meanwhile, prepare the Berry Filling: In a 4-quart saucepan, combine ½ cup raspberry-cranberry drink and 3 tablespoons cornstarch; stir in sugar and 4 cups of the blueberries. Heat the blueberry mixture to boiling over medium-high heat, stirring occasionally, until thickened. Stir in the vanilla; spoon the mixture into baked pastry shell and set aside to cool to room temperature.

5. In a 2-quart saucepan, combine remaining 1½ cups raspberry-cranberry juice drink and 2 tablespoons cornstarch until smooth. Heat to boiling, stirring constantly, until a clear pink glaze forms. Stir liqueur into glaze. Spoon ½ cup glaze into a small bowl; spoon remaining glaze into a medium-size bowl; set aside for 20 minutes.

6. Fold the raspberries into the glaze in the medium-size bowl, and the remaining 2 cups blueberries into the glaze in the small bowl. Spoon a 3-inch border of glazed raspberries around the edge of the pie over the blueberry mixture. Spoon the glazed blueberries into the center.

7. Spoon the whipped cream into a pastry bag fitted with a large star tip. Pipe whipped cream stars on the line where the raspberries and blueberries meet. Refrigerate the pie until ready to serve.

FIRST AID

When rolling out or fitting pastry into a pie pan or placing it on top of fillings, tears or holes may occur. Or you might come up short on pastry along a section of the edge of the plate. In either case, moisten the injured area with a drop of water applied with a pastry brush. Take a bit of scrap dough and press it into or onto the moistened area until the pastry is blended.

Concord Grape Pie

....

A vailable in abundance during late summer, the beautiful blue-black concord makes superb out-of-hand eating as well as wonderful jams, jellies, and pies. It is time consuming to halve and seed the little individual fruits, but for the grape lover, the deep color and confection-like aroma of this pie makes it well worth the effort. Buy bunches of full and plump grapes with a consistent color and no hint of green. Make sure they are well attached at the stems. Store, wrapped in plastic in the refrigerator, up to five days.

MAKES ONE 9-INCH PIE

Pastry for a Two-Crust Pie
  (page 83)

Grape Filling:
5 cups concord grapes, halved
  and seeded

¾ cup sugar
⅓ cup all-purpose flour
½ teaspoon ground
  cinnamon
½ teaspoon grated lemon
  rind

1. Prepare the Pastry for a Two-Crust Pie.

2. Prepare the Grape Filling: Heat the oven to 400°F. In a large bowl, combine the grapes, sugar, flour, cinnamon, and lemon rind. Toss to combine well.

3. On a lightly floured surface, roll out half the pastry into an 11-inch round. Fit the pastry into a 9-inch pie plate, leaving the edge untrimmed. Spoon the grape filling into the pastry-lined plate. Roll out the remaining pastry into a 10-inch round. With water, moisten the pastry around the rim of the pastry-lined plate. Place the pastry round on the filling; fold the edge of the top pastry under the edge of the bottom pastry so that it is even with the rim of the plate. Flute the pastry edge. With a fork, pierce the top crust to allow steam to escape during baking.

4. Bake the pie 40 to 45 minutes, or until the filling bubbles in the center. Cool completely on a wire rack before serving.

Apricot-Mincemeat Tarts

....

Here is an excellent choice for Thanksgiving dessert if you don't have a lot of baking time. It is simple, fast, and deliciously rich in the traditional holiday flavors. You can substitute dried apples, but we are partial to the color and tangy quality of the apricot.

MAKES EIGHT 3-INCH TARTS

Pastry for a Two-Crust Pie (page 83)

Apricot Filling:
⅓ cup dried apricot halves, quartered

¾ cup brandy or apricot-flavored liqueur
1 20½-ounce jar mincemeat

1. Prepare the Pastry for a Two-Crust Pie.

2. Prepare the Apricot Filling: In a small bowl, combine the apricots and ½ cup brandy. Cover and let stand 4 hours.

3. Heat the oven to 425°F. Divide the pastry into 8 balls. On a lightly floured surface, roll each ball into a 5-inch round. Fit each round into a 3-inch-wide, 1½-inch-deep tart pan. Trim the pastry even with the rim. With a fork, pierce the bottom and side of the pastry. Place the tarts on a rimmed baking sheet.

4. Bake the tart shells 10 to 12 minutes, or until golden brown. Cool the shells completely in the pans on wire racks. Remove the shells from the pans and place them on a flameproof serving tray.

5. Just before serving, in a 2-quart saucepan, combine the apricot mixture and mincemeat. Heat to boiling. Spoon the hot mixture into the shells.

6. Place the tarts on a serving cart or side table. In a long-handled metal ladle, warm the remaining ¼ cup brandy until the vapors rise. With a fireplace match, ignite the brandy and pour it over the tops of the tarts. When the flames subside, serve the tarts.

Apple and Almond Tart with Yogurt Sauce

....

R emarkably easy to prepare, this tart comes to the table a tantalizing showpiece of neatly arranged glazed apple slices atop a bed of almonds. The yogurt sauce is a rich-tasting but light complement, making this tart an unusual low-fat dessert.

Makes one 10-inch tart

Pastry for Tart or Tartlets (page 84)

Apple and Almond Filling:
7 medium-size Golden Delicious or Paula red apples, peeled, cored, and sliced
2 teaspoons lemon juice
2 tablespoons butter or margarine

Apple Glaze:
½ cup apple jelly
2 tablespoons apple brandy

¼ cup almonds, ground

Yogurt Sauce:
2 tablespoons apple brandy
1 8-ounce container vanilla yogurt

1. Prepare the Pastry for Tart or Tartlets. Heat the oven to 400°F. On a lightly floured surface, roll out the pastry into a 12-inch round. Fit the pastry into a 10-inch tart pan with a removable bottom. Trim the pastry ¼ inch above the rim of the pan and flute. Line the pastry with aluminum foil and fill with uncooked dried beans or pie weights. Bake the pastry 15 minutes. Remove the beans and foil and bake the shell 5 minutes longer. Cool the tart shell in the pan on a wire rack. Do not turn off the oven.

2. Prepare the Apple and Almond Filling: In a large bowl, toss the apples and lemon juice. In a large skillet, melt 1 tablespoon butter over medium heat. Add half the apples and saute, stirring occasionally, until tender and crisp, about 6 minutes. Remove to a large bowl; repeat with the remaining 1 tablespoon butter and the remaining apples.

3. Prepare the Apple Glaze: Heat the apple jelly over low heat just until melted. Remove from the heat. Stir in the apple brandy.

4. Sprinkle the almonds over the bottom of the tart shell. Arrange the apples over the almonds overlapping in concentric circles. Brush the apples with half the apple glaze.

5. Bake the tart 20 minutes, then remove from the oven. Heat the broiler. Brush the tart with the remaining apple glaze. Broil 4 inches from the heat until the edges of the apples are browned, 3 to 5 minutes. Cool the tart completely in the pan on the rack. Remove the side of the pan, and place the tart on a serving plate.

6. Prepare the Yogurt Sauce: In a small bowl, stir the apple brandy into the yogurt. Serve the sauce with the apple tart.

L A T T I C E - T O P   C R U S T

The lattice top is a finishing touch that gives your pie an attractive country look. Once you get the hang of interweaving the pastry strips to create the lattice-like top, you'll find that it takes very little time to add this bit of character and flair to your pies. Then you are free to experiment. Try weaving twisted strips for a more decorative finish or cutting wide strips to create a tight weave for a basket look.

On a lightly floured surface, roll out half the pastry from a two-crust recipe to a 10- by 5-inch rectangle. With a fluted pastry wheel or sharp knife, cut the rectangle lengthwise into ten ½-inch strips.

Place half of the strips evenly spaced over the filling. Leave the ends untrimmed. Fold every other strip three quarters of the way back. Place one of the remaining strips crosswise, near the edge of the pie and over the unfolded strips. Unfold the strips (they will cover the crosswise strip). Fold back an alternating set of strips. Place another crosswise strip about ¾-inch from the first crosswise strip and over the unfolded strips. Unfold the strips. Continue this weaving until the top is a woven lattice. With water, moisten the edge of the bottom pastry. Trim the ends of the strips even with the bottom pastry. Press the edges together. Fold the pastry under so that it is even with the rim of the plate and flute the edge.

Strawberry Lattice Tarts

....

Our lattice-top crust gives a simple, quick, low-calorie strawberry filling a special and upscale look.

MAKES THREE 4-INCH TARTS

*Pastry for a Two-Crust Pie
  (page 83)*

Strawberry Filling:
½ to ⅔ cup sugar
¼ cup cornstarch

*2 pint baskets (4 cups)
  strawberries, rinsed,
  hulled, and halved*
*1 tablespoon butter or
  margarine*
Milk

1. Prepare the Pastry for a Two-Crust Pie.

2. Prepare the Strawberry Filling: In a large bowl, combine ½ cup sugar and the cornstarch. Add the strawberries, tossing lightly to combine.

3. Heat the oven to 400°F. Divide each half of the pastry into 3 pieces. On a lightly floured surface, roll out 3 pieces of the pastry into 7-inch rounds. Fit each round into a 4-inch tart pan. Roll out each of the 3 remaining pieces of pastry into a 6-inch square. With a fluted pastry wheel or sharp knife, cut each square into fourteen strips, about 7/16-inch wide.

4. Divide the strawberry mixture among the tart pans and dot with butter. To make a lattice top crust, place 7 strips evenly spaced over the top of the filling of one tart. Leave the ends untrimmed. Fold every other strip three-quarters of the way back. Place one of the remaining strips crosswise, near the edge of the tart and over the unfolded strips. Unfold the strips (they will cover the crosswise strip). Fold back a set of alternating strips. Place another crosswise strip next to the first crosswise strip and over the unfolded strips. Unfold the strips. Continue weaving 5 more strips until the top is a woven lattice. With water, moisten the edge of the bottom pastry. Fold the overhang of the bottom pastry over the ends of the strips and flute. Repeat with the remaining 2 tarts. Brush the lattice tops, but not the piecrust edges, lightly with milk.

5. Bake the tarts 40 minutes, or until the filling bubbles in the center. Cool on wire racks.

Coffee-Walnut Tart

···········

In the tradition of the great French pastry chefs, we have combined a smooth coffee-flavor filling with the sweet-spirited walnut. Use instant espresso powder for a more pronounced coffee flavor. Toasting the walnuts lightly will enhance their flavor a great deal and add even more richness to this tart.

MAKES ONE 11-INCH TART

*Pastry for a Two-Crust Pie
    (page 83)*

Coffee Walnut Filling:
4 eggs
⅓ cup instant coffee powder
½ cup granulated sugar
*½ cup firmly packed
    light-brown sugar*
½ cup light corn syrup

*1 tablespoon all-purpose
    flour*
1 teaspoon vanilla extract
¼ teaspoon salt
*2 tablespoons butter or
    margarine, melted*
1½ cups walnut pieces

Whipped cream (optional)

1. Prepare the Pastry for a Two-Crust Pie, except divide the pastry into 2 portions, one slightly larger than the other. On a lightly floured surface, roll out the larger portion of the pastry into a 14-inch round. Save remaining pastry for use at another time. Fit the pastry into an 11-inch fluted tart pan with a removable bottom. Trim the pastry even with rim of the pan.

2. Prepare the Coffee Walnut Filling: Heat the oven to 350°F. In a medium-size bowl, with an electric mixer on high speed, beat the eggs and coffee until the mixture is frothy and the coffee dissolves. Reduce the mixer speed to low, and beat in the granulated sugar, brown sugar, corn syrup, flour, vanilla, and salt until well combined. Stir in the butter. Pour the mixture into the pastry-lined pan. Sprinkle the walnuts over the filling. Place the tart pan on a rimmed baking sheet.

3. Bake the tart 55 to 60 minutes, or until the center stays firm when the tart is gently shaken. Cool the tart on a wire rack. Just before serving, remove the side of the pan and place the tart on a serving plate. If desired, decorate the tart with whipped cream.

Chocolate-Orange Rice Tart

....

A n Italian classic, this tart is higher than most, more like the size of a cake. Its irresistible creamy texture is due to smooth ricotta cheese and Arborio rice. Both are available in specialty Italian food stores and we strongly recommend that you use no substitutes. This tart is best served warm, or at room temperature.

MAKES ONE 9-INCH TART

Sweet Crust Pastry:
2 cups all-purpose flour
⅓ cup granulated sugar
¼ teaspoon baking powder
¼ teaspoon salt
½ cup (1 stick) butter or
    margarine, slightly softened
1 egg
3 tablespoons water

Ricotta-Rice Filling:
½ cup Arborio rice
½ teaspoon salt

½ cup granulated sugar
2 cups milk
8 ounces part-skim ricotta
    cheese
4 eggs
1 teaspoon vanilla extract
½ teaspoon finely grated
    orange rind

¼ cup semisweet chocolate
    mini chips

Confectioners' sugar

1. Prepare the Sweet Crust Pastry: In a large bowl, combine the flour, ⅓ cup granulated sugar, baking powder, and salt. With a pastry blender or 2 knives, cut the butter into the flour mixture until the mixture resembles coarse crumbs. In a small bowl, beat the egg and water. Stir the beaten egg into the flour mixture until the mixture holds together. Shape the pastry into 2 balls, one slightly larger than the other. Wrap and refrigerate the pastry at least 30 minutes.

2. Prepare the Ricotta-Rice Filling: In a 2½-quart saucepan, heat 2 quarts water to boiling over high heat; stir in the rice and salt. Return the mixture to boiling. Reduce the heat and simmer 20 minutes; drain the rice well.

3. In the same saucepan, combine the drained rice, ½ cup sugar, and milk; heat the mixture to boiling over high heat. Reduce the heat and simmer, stirring frequently, until the mixture is very thick and creamy, about 25 minutes. Remove from the heat; set aside.

4. In a food processor fitted with the chopping blade, process the ricotta until very smooth, or press the ricotta through a fine mesh strainer. In a large bowl, with an electric mixer on low speed, combine the ricotta and the rice mixture. Increase the mixer speed to medium. Add the eggs, one at a time, beating well after each addition. Beat in the vanilla and orange rind. Set aside.

5. Heat the oven to 375°F. On a lightly floured surface, roll out the larger ball of pastry into a 13-inch round. Fit the pastry into a 9-inch springform pan, lining the bottom and side. On a lightly floured surface, roll out the remaining ball of pastry into a 9- by 6-inch rectangle. Trim the edges even all around. With a fluted pastry wheel or sharp knife, cut the rectangle into five 1-inch-wide strips.

6. Pour the filling into the pastry-lined pan; sprinkle the chocolate chips evenly on top (do not stir into the filling). Place the 5 pastry strips, evenly spaced, on the filling; crimp the ends to the rim to prevent them from sinking into the filling.

7. Bake the tart 45 to 50 minutes, or until the center remains firm when the pie is gently shaken. Cool the tart in the pan on a wire rack for 20 minutes. Remove the side of the pan, and place the tart on a serving plate. Sift confectioners' sugar lightly over the top and serve.

T I P S   O N   T A R T S :
F I N I S H I N G   T O U C H E S

Glazing: Fresh fruit tarts intensify in color and luster when a glaze of melted jelly is brushed on the top as a finishing touch. Leftover glaze keeps refrigerated in a covered container several months. To use again, reheat and thin with water.

Unmolding: Most tarts are baked in pans with removable bottoms and served in their delicate crusts. To unmold, place the cooled tart on a wide-mouthed can or jar. Gently slip the fluted ring down the side of the tart. If the ring doesn't move easily, use the point of a knife to carefully work it loose.

Apple Cheese Tart

....

Ground almonds and a splash of almond extract create the distinct character and flavor of this creamy tart. A circle of glazed unpeeled red apple slices provides a treat for the eyes.

MAKES ONE 10-INCH TART

Pastry for Tart or Tartlets
 (page 84)

Apple Cheese Filling:
3 medium-size red baking
 apples, unpeeled, cored,
 and sliced
2 teaspoons lemon juice
½ pound farmer or dry curd
 cheese
¼ cup sugar
1 egg, separated, at room
 temperature

1 cup unsweetened
 applesauce
⅓ cup ground almonds
2 tablespoons lemon juice
½ teaspoon grated lemon
 rind
¼ teaspoon almond extract
1 tablespoon butter or
 margarine, melted

¼ cup apricot preserves

1. Prepare the Pastry for Tart or Tartlets. Heat the oven to 400°F. On a lightly floured surface, roll out the pastry into a 12-inch round. Fit the pastry into a 10-inch fluted tart pan with a removable bottom. Trim the pastry even with the rim. Line the pastry with aluminum foil and fill with uncooked dried beans or pie weights. Bake the pastry 10 to 15 minutes. Remove the beans and foil, and cool the partially baked tart shell on a wire rack.

2. Prepare the Apple Cheese Filling: Reduce the oven temperature to 350°F. In a medium-size bowl, combine the apples and 2 teaspoons lemon juice; toss to coat well. Set aside. In a large bowl, with an electric mixer on medium speed, mix the cheese, sugar, and egg yolk until smooth. Stir in the applesauce, almonds, 2 tablespoons lemon juice, lemon rind, and almond extract. In a small bowl, with clean beaters and the mixer on high speed, beat the egg white until stiff; fold into the cheese mixture. Pour the mixture into the prepared crust.

3. Arrange the apple slices, overlapping, in concentric circles on top of the cheese mixture. Brush the apples with butter.

4. Bake the tart 35 minutes, or until the pastry is golden, the cheese mixture is set, and the apples are tender and light brown. Cool the tart completely in the pan on the rack. In a small saucepan, heat the apricot preserves over low heat until melted. Brush the apples with the warm preserves. To serve, remove the side of the pan and place the tart on a serving plate. Refrigerate any remaining tart.

Heart-Shaped Strawberry Tarts

A perfect dessert to celebrate love! Beg, borrow, or buy heart-shaped molds so you can make these sweet passionate tarts.

MAKES EIGHT 3-INCH TARTS

Pastry for a Two-Crust Pie
(page 83)

Cream Filling:
½ cup (¼ pint) heavy cream

¼ cup almond macaroon
crumbs (about 6 macaroons)

1 pint basket (2 cups) small
strawberries
¼ cup strawberry jelly

1. Prepare the Pastry for a Two-Crust Pie, except divide the pastry into 8 pieces. Heat oven to 425°F.
2. On a lightly floured surface, roll out each piece of pastry into a 5-inch round. Fit each round into a 3-inch, heart-shaped ovenproof mold. Trim the pastry even with the rim of the mold. With a fork, pierce the bottoms and sides of the pastry. Bake the tart shells 15 to 17 minutes, or until golden. Cool the tart shells in the molds on wire racks.
3. Prepare the Cream Filling: In a small bowl, with an electric mixer on medium speed, beat the cream until stiff peaks form. Fold the macaroon crumbs into the cream. Remove the tart shells from the molds and place on a serving tray. Divide the cream mixture among the tart shells.
4. Rinse and hull the strawberries; drain well on paper towels. In a small saucepan, heat the jelly over medium heat until melted. Divide the strawberries among the tart shells. Brush the strawberries with jelly.

Cherry Cobbler

....

A n American dessert since Colonial days, cobblers are easy to assemble and a quick way to use an abundance of fresh fruit. This deepdish cherry mix is topped with a sweet crust, and is best served when still warm. Try a scoop of ice cream alongside.

MAKES ONE 2-QUART COBBLER

Cherry Filling:
4 cups fresh sour cherries,
    pitted
2½ tablespoons cornstarch
½ teaspoon ground nutmeg
¼ cup granulated sugar

1½ teaspoons baking powder
6 tablespoons (¾ stick)
    butter or margarine,
    cut into chunks
1 egg
¼ cup milk

·Cobbler Pastry:
1½ cups all-purpose flour
2 tablespoons light-brown
    sugar

1 egg yolk, beaten with 1
    tablespoon water
    (optional)

1. Prepare the Cherry Filling: Heat the oven to 375°F. Grease a shallow 2-quart baking dish. In a medium-size bowl, combine the cherries, cornstarch, nutmeg, and granulated sugar. Spoon the cherry mixture into the baking dish.

2. Prepare the Cobbler Pastry: In a medium-size bowl, combine the flour, brown sugar, and baking powder. With a pastry blender or 2 knives, cut the butter into the flour mixture until the mixture resembles coarse crumbs.

3. In a small bowl, beat the egg and milk. Stir the egg mixture into the flour mixture and mix until the pastry holds together when lightly pressed. Turn onto a lightly floured surface and knead lightly. Pat the pastry into a shape to fit the baking dish. Place over the cherries. With a knife, pierce the pastry to allow steam to escape during baking. If desired, brush the top with the beaten egg yolk.

4. Bake the cobbler 30 to 35 minutes, or until the filling bubbles in the center. Cool on a wire rack for 10 minutes and serve warm, or cool the cobbler completely and serve at room temperature.

Orange Custard Tart, page 44

Three-Berry Tart, page 38

Pumpkin Brûlée Tarts

....

These are creamy holiday tarts made ahead and kept cold until just before serving, when they are drizzled with a hot sugar glaze.

MAKES FOUR 4-INCH TARTS

Pastry for Tart or Tartlets
(page 84)

Pumpkin Filling:
1 cup canned pumpkin or
fresh pumpkin puree
2 eggs
⅓ cup heavy cream
¼ cup maple syrup

½ teaspoon grated, peeled,
fresh gingerroot
½ teaspoon ground cinnamon
¼ teaspoon ground nutmeg
¼ teaspoon salt

Brûlée Glaze:
½ cup sugar
3 tablespoons water

1. Prepare the Pastry for Tart or Tartlets.

2. Prepare the Pumpkin Filling: In a medium-size bowl, with an electric mixer on medium speed, beat the pumpkin, eggs, cream, maple syrup, gingerroot, cinnamon, nutmeg, and salt until well combined. Refrigerate the filling while preparing the tart shells.

3. Heat the oven to 425°F. Divide the pastry into 4 pieces and shape into balls. On a lightly floured surface, roll out each piece of pastry into a 6-inch round. Fit each round into a 4-inch tart pan. Trim the pastry even with the rim of the pan.

4. Divide the pumpkin filling among the tarts. Bake the tarts for 10 minutes. Reduce the oven temperature to 350°F, and bake 20 to 25 minutes longer, or until the centers appear firm and puffed. Cool the tarts in the pans on a wire rack 15 minutes. Cover and refrigerate the tarts until well chilled.

5. To serve, remove the sides of the pans and place the tarts on a serving plate. Prepare the Brûlée Glaze: In a small saucepan, combine the sugar and water. Cook over low heat, stirring constantly and washing down sugar particles from the side of the pan with a wet brush, until the sugar is dissolved. Increase the heat and boil, without stirring, until the mixture turns dark golden, 10 minutes. Remove from the heat and let stand just 1 minute. Drizzle the tops of the tarts with the brûlée glaze and serve immediately.

Three-Berry Tart

PHOTOGRAPH ON PAGE 36

Here is an extremely light and satisfying summer tart. We have chosen raspberries as a flavor base. For the strawberries or blueberries, you can substitute blackberries, boysenberries, or any good-tasting wild berry that may grow in your part of the country.

MAKES ONE 9-INCH TART

Lemon Pastry:
1 ¼ cups all-purpose flour
2 tablespoons sugar
1 teaspoon grated lemon rind
¼ teaspoon salt
⅓ cup vegetable shortening
3 to 4 tablespoons ice water

Berry Filling:
Water
1 10-ounce package quick-
thawing frozen raspber-
ries, thawed and well
drained, syrup reserved

1 ½ tablespoons cornstarch
2 tablespoons orange-flavored
liqueur or 1 tablespoon
sugar
1 pint basket (2 cups)
strawberries, rinsed,
hulled, and halved
1 ½ cups fresh blueberries
½ cup fresh raspberries

Whipped cream (optional)

1. Prepare the Lemon Pastry: Heat the oven to 400°F. In a medium-size bowl, combine the flour, sugar, lemon rind, and salt. With a pastry blender or 2 knives, cut the shortening into the flour mixture until the mixture resembles coarse crumbs. Stir in the ice water, 1 tablespoon at a time, and mix just until the mixture holds together. Shape the pastry into a ball. On a lightly floured surface, roll out the ball into an 11-inch round. Fit the pastry into a 9-inch fluted tart pan with a removable bottom. Trim the pastry even with the rim of the pan.

2. With a fork, pierce the bottom and side of the tart shell. Line the tart shell with aluminum foil and fill with uncooked dried beans or pie weights. Bake the shell for 10 minutes, or until golden. Remove the beans and foil from the tart shell. Bake the tart shell 5 to 10 minutes longer, or until lightly browned. Cool completely in the pan on a wire rack.

3. Roll out the pastry scraps. If desired, with a cookie cutter or sharp knife, cut out 3 ivy-leaf shapes. Score the leaves with lines to resemble

veins. Roll a small piece of pastry between fingers to form a tendril. Prop the leaves over a small piece of aluminum foil to make them curl. Place the leaves on a baking sheet or piece of aluminum foil. Bake 10 minutes or until golden. Cool on a wire rack.

4. Prepare the Berry Filling: Add water to the reserved raspberry syrup to make 1 cup. In a 1-quart saucepan, combine the cornstarch and raspberry syrup until smooth. Heat to boiling over medium heat, stirring constantly; cook until thickened and clear. Stir in the liqueur.

5. Set aside ¾ cup of the raspberry sauce. Fold the raspberries into the remaining sauce. Remove the tart shell from the pan and place on a serving plate. Spread the sauce with raspberries evenly over the bottom of the tart shell.

6. Arrange a double circle of strawberries around the outer edge of the tart, then a circle of blueberries. Place the fresh raspberries in the center of the tart. Glaze the top of the tart with the reserved ¾ cup raspberry sauce. Arrange the pastry leaves around the edge of the tart. Refrigerate the tart at least 1 hour before serving. Serve with whipped cream, if desired.

PIES AND TARTS THE NEXT DAY: STORING

Most creamy pies and tarts have more flavor at a moderate temperature, but delicate cream and chiffon fillings can spoil if left too long at room temperature. For safe keeping, cover cooled pies and tarts with plastic wrap and refrigerate them. Allow 30 minutes for the chilled pie to come to room temperature. Fruit pies and cobblers, on the other hand, should be kept at room temperature, loosely covered with plastic wrap. Refrigerated, the flavor of the fruit dulls and the crust becomes soggy. You can't recapture the lost flavor, but you can recrisp a soggy crust in a 400°F oven for 10 minutes.

Pear-Cranberry Cobbler

....

New Englanders love mixing their native cranberries with pears. Both Bosc and Seckel pears are at peak flavor during fall. This seasonal favorite is topped with a traditional drop-biscuit crust, and most often served with ice cream.

MAKES ONE 1½-QUART COBBLER

Pear Filling:
1 tablespoon butter or
margarine
5 medium-size pears, peeled,
cored, and cut into
½-inch chunks
1 cup fresh or thawed frozen
cranberries
⅓ cup firmly packed
dark-brown sugar
⅓ cup granulated sugar
3 tablespoons cornstarch
2 tablespoons lemon juice

2 teaspoons ground
cinnamon
½ teaspoon ground ginger

Biscuit Topping:
1 cup all-purpose flour
¼ cup granulated sugar
1 teaspoon baking powder
2 tablespoons milk
1 egg, lightly beaten
¼ cup (½ stick) butter,
melted

Vanilla ice cream (optional)

1. Prepare the Pear Filling: In a large skillet, melt the butter over medium heat. Add the pears and saute until slightly softened, about 3 minutes. Remove the skillet from the heat and stir in the cranberries, brown sugar, ⅓ cup granulated sugar, cornstarch, lemon juice, cinnamon, and ginger. Spoon the pear filling into a 1½-quart baking dish.

2. Prepare the Biscuit Topping: Heat the oven to 325°F. In a large bowl, combine the flour, ¼ cup granulated sugar, and baking powder. Stir in the milk and egg just until the mixture is moistened. Stir in the butter. Spoon the biscuit topping over the pear filling. Place the cobbler on a rimmed baking sheet.

3. Bake the cobbler 55 to 60 minutes, or until the top is browned and the filling bubbles. Cool slightly on a wire rack. Serve warm with vanilla ice cream, if desired.

Nectarine-Kiwi-Pistachio Tart

If you've always wanted to make a tart like those at fine patisseries, this is the one. Glistening and glazed, thin slices of fruit on a sumptuous pistachio-nut crust make this tart a treat for the eyes and a delightful experience for the palate. In this recipe, do not substitute a tart pan for the springform pan.

MAKES ONE 9-INCH TART

Pistachio Crust:
½ cup (1 stick) unsalted
  butter, softened
½ cup sugar
2 eggs
¾ cup shelled unsalted
  pistachios, finely ground
½ cup all-purpose flour
Pinch of salt

Fruit Filling:
¼ cup apple jelly
2 large nectarines, halved,
  pitted, and thinly sliced
2 large kiwifruit, peeled,
  trimmed, and thinly sliced
¼ cup seedless red grapes,
  halved

1. Heat the oven to 375°F. Grease a 9-inch springform pan, and line the bottom with waxed paper; lightly grease and flour the paper.

2. Prepare the Pistachio Crust: In a large bowl, with an electric mixer on medium speed, beat the butter and sugar until light and fluffy. Add the eggs, one at a time, beating well after each addition. Reduce the mixer speed to low, and beat in the pistachios, flour, and salt. Spread the batter evenly in the prepared pan. Bake the pistachio crust 20 to 25 minutes, or until golden brown. Cool the crust completely in the pan on a wire rack.

3. Prepare the Fruit Filling: Just before serving, in a small saucepan, heat the jelly over low heat until melted. Remove the side of the pan from the pistachio crust. Invert the crust onto a serving plate; remove the bottom of the pan and the waxed paper. Brush the top and side of the crust with some melted jelly.

4. Arrange the nectarine slices, overlapping, in a concentric circle around the top edge of the crust. Arrange the kiwi slices in another circle toward the center of the tart. Arrange the grape halves, cut sides down, in the center of the tart. Brush the fruit with the remaining warm jelly. Serve immediately, or refrigerate up to 4 hours before serving.

Lattice Lemon Meringue Tarts

....

A meringue latticework is piped onto these light and summery individual desserts. They're perfect for Sunday brunch or a porch supper.

MAKES FOUR 4-INCH TARTS

Poppy Seed Pastry:
1 cup all-purpose flour
2 teaspoons sugar
1 teaspoon poppy seeds
¼ teaspoon salt
6 tablespoons (¾ stick)
   butter or margarine, chilled
2 to 3 tablespoons cold
   water

Lemon Filling:
½ cup water

⅓ cup lemon juice
½ cup sugar
3 tablespoons cornstarch
1 teaspoon grated lemon rind
2 egg yolks (reserve the egg
   whites for the meringue)

Meringue:
2 egg whites, at room
   temperature
¼ teaspoon cream of tartar
3 tablespoons sugar

1. Prepare the Poppy Seed Pastry: In a medium-size bowl, combine the flour, sugar, poppy seeds, and salt. With a pastry blender or 2 knives, cut the butter into the flour mixture until the mixture resembles coarse crumbs. Stir in the cold water, 1 tablespoon at a time, and mix lightly until the mixture holds together. Shape the pastry into 4 balls. Wrap and refrigerate at least 30 minutes.

2. Heat the oven to 400°F. On a lightly floured surface, roll out each ball into a 5-inch round. Fit each round into a 4-inch fluted tart pan with a removable bottom. Trim the pastry even with the rim of the pan. With a fork, pierce the bottoms and sides of the pastry. Bake the tart shells 15 to 20 minutes, or until lightly browned. Cool the shells completely in the pans on a wire rack.

3. Prepare the Lemon Filling: In a 2-quart saucepan, combine the water, lemon juice, sugar, cornstarch, and lemon rind. Heat to boiling over high heat, stirring constantly. Reduce heat to medium; cook, stirring constantly, until the mixture thickens, about 3 minutes.

4. In a medium-size bowl, beat the egg yolks. Slowly beat the hot lemon mixture into the egg yolks; pour all the mixture back into the saucepan. Cook over low heat, stirring constantly, until the filling

is heated through but not boiling, 2 minutes. Pour the lemon filling into the tart shells. Place the tarts on a baking sheet until cool.

5. Prepare the Meringue: In a small bowl, with an electric mixer on high speed, beat the egg whites and cream of tartar until foamy. Gradually add the sugar, beating until stiff peaks form.

6. Heat the broiler. Spoon the meringue into a pastry bag fitted with a star tip. On the top of each tart, pipe 3 lines of meringue evenly spaced in one direction, then pipe 3 lines crisscrossing in the opposite direction. Place the tarts 4 inches from the heat and broil until the meringue is lightly browned, about 2 minutes. Cool the tarts in the pans 15 minutes. Remove the sides of the pans and place the tarts on a serving plate.

TEST-KITCHEN TIPS

Meringue toppings are delicate, air-filled mixtures of egg white and sugar and should be made shortly before serving the pie or tart. Spread or pipe the topping over the filling, to the edge of the pie. (Egg white contains a protein that will shrink with heat, but when the meringue adheres to the edge, it will not pull away during baking.)

For that pastry-shop look, add a glaze to the top crust. Be forewarned that a glaze may also toughen the crust slightly. To ensure golden color, brush the pastry with melted butter, milk, or a mixture of sugar and milk before baking. For color and gloss, brush the pastry with egg yolk that has been lightly beaten with a tablespoon of water just before baking. If, during baking, the crust browns too quickly, cover the edges or top lightly with aluminum foil. Bake fruit pies and tarts on a rimmed baking sheet in case juices bubble over.

Do not overbake silky and translucent custard pies. This is the most common cause of the cracks that occur on the top of pumpkin, lemon, and pecan pies. Bake only until the center is just barely firm and it jiggles slightly when the pan is gently shaken. The pie continues to bake as it cools, but without drying or cracking.

Orange Custard Tart
PHOTOGRAPH ON PAGE 35

We suggest you use navel oranges for this pretty tart. They are sweet and contain no seeds. For ease and convenience, all but the last decorative steps can be done a day ahead. When you do finish the tart, allow it to sit at room temperature at least 30 minutes before serving to perk up the orange flavors.

MAKES ONE 9-INCH TART

Baked Tart Shell
(page 82)

Glazed Oranges:
2 small oranges, rinsed,
dried, and thinly sliced
⅔ cup orange marmalade
2 tablespoons orange juice

Custard Filling:
½ cup sugar
⅓ cup cornstarch
¼ teaspoon salt
2 cups (1 pint) half-and-half
2 eggs
1½ teaspoons grated orange
rind

1. Prepare the Baked Tart Shell.

2. Prepare the Glazed Oranges: Cut the orange slices in half. In a medium-size skillet, heat the marmalade and orange juice over medium heat. Add half the oranges to the marmalade; cook, turning once, until glazed, 15 to 20 minutes. With a slotted spoon, remove the oranges to a lightly greased plate. Repeat with the remaining oranges. Cover the oranges and refrigerate. Reserve the remaining marmalade mixture.

3. Prepare the Custard Filling: In a small saucepan, combine the sugar, cornstarch, and salt. Gradually stir in the half-and-half. Heat the mixture to boiling over medium heat, stirring constantly; cook 1 minute. In a small bowl, combine the eggs and orange rind. Stir half the hot mixture into the eggs; stir all the egg mixture back into the mixture in the saucepan. Cook over low heat, stirring constantly, just until thickened. Do not boil.

4. Pour the filling into the tart shell. Cool the tart on a wire rack for 30 minutes. Cover and refrigerate until chilled. One hour before serving, arrange the orange slices on top of the filling. Brush the tart with the reserved marmalade mixture.

Peach Cobbler

....

This is an old-fashioned dessert with a sweet, substantial, biscuit-like topping. An old baker's trick for enhancing the flavors of unimpressive-tasting fresh peaches is to add a pinch or two of ground mace to the filling before baking.

MAKES ONE 2-QUART COBBLER

Peach Filling:
9 medium-size peaches,
    peeled, halved, pitted, and
    sliced, or 6 cups drained,
    thawed frozen peach slices
1 tablespoon lemon juice
¼ cup firmly packed light-
    brown sugar
1½ tablespoons cornstarch
½ cup water

Topping:
½ cup granulated sugar
½ cup all-purpose flour
½ teaspoon baking powder
¼ teaspoon salt
2 tablespoons butter or
    margarine, softened
1 egg

Granulated sugar (optional)

1. Prepare the Peach Filling: Heat the oven to 400°F. Lightly grease a 2-quart casserole. Place the peach slices in the casserole and gently toss with the lemon juice.

2. In a 1-quart saucepan, combine the brown sugar and cornstarch. Stir in the water, stirring until the cornstarch dissolves. Cook over medium heat, stirring constantly, until the sauce thickens, about 5 minutes. Pour the sauce over the peaches in the casserole.

3. Prepare the Topping: Set aside 1 teaspoon granulated sugar. In a medium-size bowl, combine the remaining granulated sugar, the flour, baking powder, and salt. Stir in the butter and egg to make a soft dough. Drop spoonfuls of the dough onto the peach filling (the topping will spread as it bakes). Sprinkle with the 1 teaspoon granulated sugar.

4. Bake the cobbler 40 to 45 minutes, or until the topping is golden brown and the filling bubbles in the center. Cool on a wire rack. Sprinkle with additional granulated sugar, if desired, and serve the cobbler warm or at room temperature.

Cranberry Meringue Pie

....

The contrast of light meringue and deep-red cranberry filling is not only stunning to look at but the sweet topping complements the slightly tart berry exquisitely. On Thanksgiving, Christmas, or anytime, this is a splendid way to feature the cranberry at your holiday feast.

MAKES ONE 10-INCH PIE

Pastry:
1⅓ cups all-purpose flour
1 tablespoon instant nonfat
  dry milk powder
½ teaspoon salt
½ cup vegetable shortening
3 to 4 tablespoons ice water

Cranberry Filling:
1¼ cups sugar
3 tablespoons cornstarch
¾ cup water

2 tablespoons lemon juice
1 teaspoon grated lemon rind
¼ teaspoon salt
2 12-ounce packages fresh
  cranberries, rinsed and
  picked over

Meringue:
4 egg whites, at room
  temperature
½ teaspoon cream of tartar
½ cup sugar

1. Prepare the Pastry: In a medium-size bowl, combine the flour, milk powder, and salt. With a pastry blender or 2 knives, cut the shortening into the flour mixture until the mixture resembles very coarse crumbs. Stir in the ice water, 1 tablespoon at a time, just until the pastry holds together. Shape the pastry into a ball. Wrap and refrigerate at least 30 minutes.

2. Heat the oven to 400°F. On a lightly floured surface, roll out the pastry into a 12-inch round. Fit the pastry into a 10-inch pie plate. Fold the edge of the pastry under so that it is even with the rim of the plates; flute the pastry edge. With a fork, pierce the bottom and side of the pastry. Bake the pastry 15 minutes, or until golden. Cool slightly on a wire rack.

3. Prepare the Cranberry Filling: In a 2-quart saucepan, combine the sugar and cornstarch. Gradually stir in the water, lemon juice, lemon

rind, and salt. Heat to boiling over medium heat, stirring constantly. Add the cranberries; cook until the cranberries start to pop, 5 to 8 minutes. Pour the filling into the baked piecrust.

4. Reduce the oven to 350°F. Prepare the Meringue: In a small bowl, with an electric mixer on high speed, beat the egg whites and cream of tartar until soft peaks form. Very gradually add the sugar, beating until stiff peaks form. Spread the meringue over the cranberry filling sealing to the edge of the crust. Bake the pie 8 to 10 minutes, or until the meringue is golden brown. Cool on the wire rack.

Sweet Potato Pie

A Southern tradition, this pie has versions as numerous as the towns from North Carolina to the Mississippi Delta. When buying sweet potatoes, choose small to medium dark-skinned ones (not the pale variety) with unbruised skins. Cook them in boiling water in their jackets; peel and puree until smooth.

MAKES ONE 9-INCH PIE

Unbaked 9-inch Piecrust
  (page 82)

Sweet Potato Filling:
2 cups well-drained sweet
  potato puree

1 14-ounce can sweetened
  condensed milk (not
  evaporated milk)
2 eggs
1 tablespoon vanilla extract
¼ teaspoon salt

1. Prepare the Unbaked 9-inch Piecrust, making sure the edge is a high scalloped flute.

2. Prepare the Sweet Potato Filling: Heat the oven to 350°F. In a medium-size bowl, beat the sweet potato puree, condensed milk, eggs, vanilla, and salt until smooth. Pour the sweet potato filling into the piecrust. Place the pie on a rimmed baking sheet.

3. Bake the pie 60 to 65 minutes, or until the center appears firm when the pie is gently shaken. Cool on a wire rack.

Cambridge Sour Cream Apple Pie

....

A dressed-up version of a traditional English country pie, this one has a nut-crunch topping over a creamy apple filling and a lattice-top crust. It's perfect for any holiday table.

MAKES ONE 9-INCH PIE

Pastry for a Two-Crust Pie
    (page 83)

Sour Cream Apple Filling:
1 cup (½ pint) sour cream
½ cup granulated sugar
1 egg
¼ teaspoon salt
1 teaspoon vanilla extract
3 tablespoons all-purpose
    flour

5 medium-size tart baking
    apples, peeled, cored, and
    thinly sliced

Cinnamon-Walnut Topping:
⅓ cup firmly packed
    light-brown sugar
1 teaspoon ground cinnamon
1 cup finely chopped walnuts
    or pecans

1. Prepare the Pastry for a Two-Crust Pie. On a lightly floured surface, roll out half the pastry into an 11-inch round. Fit the pastry into a 9-inch pie plate, leaving the edge untrimmed.

2. Prepare the Sour Cream Apple Filling: Heat the oven to 375°F. In a large bowl, with an electric mixer on medium speed, beat the sour cream, granulated sugar, egg, salt, vanilla, and flour until well blended. Add the apples and stir to coat well. Spoon the filling into the pastry-lined plate.

3. Prepare the Cinnamon-Walnut Topping: In a small bowl, combine the brown sugar, cinnamon, and walnuts, and sprinkle the topping evenly over the apple mixture. Top with the lattice crust, page 27.

4. Bake the pie 50 minutes, or until the filling bubbles in the center. Serve the pie warm, or cool completely on a wire rack and serve at room temperature.

Deep-Dish Mincemeat Pie

....

This is an ample and festive pie. Not all prepared mincemeats are alike. Experiment until you find one your family prefers.

MAKES 10-INCH PIE

Pastry for a Two-Crust Pie
(page 83)

Mincemeat Filling:
1 28-ounce jar prepared
mincemeat
2 large or 3 medium-size
Winesap or Rome apples,
peeled, cored, and coarsely
chopped

2 tablespoons Cognac or
brandy
1 tablespoon rum (optional)
½ teaspoon ground black
pepper
½ pound ground smoked
ham, cooked sausage,
cooked venison, or cooked
beef heart

1 egg, beaten

1. Prepare the Pastry for a Two-Crust Pie.

2. Prepare the Mincemeat Filling: In a large bowl, combine the mincemeat, apples, Cognac, rum, if desired, pepper, and ham.

3. On lightly floured waxed paper, roll out half the pastry into a 12-inch round. Fit the pastry into a 10-inch deep-dish pie plate.

4. Heat the oven to 400°F. Brush the pastry with some of the egg to seal it against the filling's juices. Roll out the remaining pastry into a 11-inch round. With a fluted pastry wheel or sharp knife, cut the round into 1-inch-wide strips.

5. Spoon the mincemeat filling into the pastry-lined plate. Top with lattice crust, page 27. Brush the strips with the remaining egg.

6. Bake the pie 30 to 40 minutes, or until the crust is browned and the filling is heated throughout. Serve the pie warm.

In 16th-Century England, cooks mixed minced venison with spirits as a preservative. A dessert was born when fruit and nuts were added to the mixture.

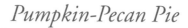

Pumpkin-Pecan Pie

Some say the secret to good pumpkin pie is not the pumpkin but the spice. Our recipe calls for your favorite pumpkin-pie spice. If you don't have one and want to use ours, combine 1 teaspoon cinnamon, ½ teaspoon ground ginger, ¼ teaspoon freshly ground nutmeg and ¼ teaspoon ground cloves.

MAKES TWO 9-INCH PIES

Pastry for a Two-Crust Pie (page 83)

Pumpkin Filling:
2 eggs, separated, at room temperature
½ cup sugar
1 16-ounce can pumpkin, or 2 cups well-drained fresh pumpkin puree
½ cup half-and-half

2 teaspoons pumpkin-pie spice
½ teaspoon salt

Pecan Filling:
3 tablespoons butter or margarine
½ cup sugar
1 cup dark corn syrup
1 teaspoon vanilla extract
2 eggs
2 cups pecan halves

1. Prepare the Pastry for a Two-Crust Pie. On a lightly floured surface, roll out half the pastry into an 11-inch round. Fit the pastry into a 9-inch pie plate. Fold the pastry overhang under, so that it extends slightly beyond the rim; flute a high pastry edge. Repeat with the other half of the pastry in another 9-inch pie plate. Refrigerate the pastry-lined plates while preparing the fillings.

2. Heat the oven to 350°F. Prepare the Pumpkin Filling: In a small bowl, with an electric mixer on high speed, beat the egg whites until soft peaks form. Gradually add the sugar, beating until stiff, glossy peaks form. In a large bowl, with the same beaters and the mixer on low speed, beat the egg yolks, pumpkin, half-and-half, pumpkin-pie spice, and salt until blended. Gently fold the egg whites into the pumpkin mixture. Divide the pumpkin filling between the prepared pastry-lined plates. Bake the pies 30 minutes.

3. Meanwhile, prepare the Pecan Filling: In a 1-quart saucepan, melt the butter over low heat. Remove the saucepan from the heat. Stir in

the sugar, corn syrup, and vanilla until blended. Stir in the eggs.

4. Remove the pies from the oven. Carefully arrange the pecan halves in a single layer in concentric circles on the pumpkin filling. Gently pour the sugar mixture over the pecans.

5. Bake the pies 15 to 20 minutes longer, or until a knife inserted 1 inch from the edge comes out clean. Cool the pies completely on wire racks before serving. Refrigerate any remaining pie.

Chess Pie

············

This creamy pie originated in England, but got its popular name, some say, from a Southern waitress. When asked what was for dessert one day, she said, "Jes' Pie." When asked to explain, she said, "It's not apple, not berry, not peach pie. It's jes' pie." Jes' became Chess and the pie became a Southern favorite.

MAKES ONE 9-INCH PIE

*Unbaked 9-inch Piecrust
   (page 82)*

Filling:
1 cup sugar
3 tablespoons cornstarch

6 eggs
⅔ cup lemon juice
*5 tablespoons butter, melted
   and cooled*
*1 tablespoon grated
   lemon rind*

1. Prepare the Unbaked 9-inch Piecrust.

2. Prepare the Filling: Heat the oven to 325°F. In a large bowl, combine the sugar and cornstarch. With an electric mixer on medium speed, add the eggs, one at a time, beating well after each addition. Stir the lemon juice and butter into the egg mixture until blended. Stir in the lemon rind. Pour the mixture into the prepared piecrust.

3. Bake the pie 50 minutes, or until a knife inserted about 1 inch from the edge comes out clean. Cool the pie completely on a wire rack before serving.

Four-Nut Pie

PHOTOGRAPH ON PAGE 53

This pie is a nut lover's fantasy, packed with a rich combination of America's abundant nut orchards — filberts from the Northwest, almonds and walnuts from the West, and pecans from the South. This is a multiregional dessert.

MAKES ONE 9-INCH PIE

Unbaked 9-inch Piecrust
(page 82)

Four-Nut Filling:
1 cup walnut halves
⅔ cup pecan halves
½ cup whole hazelnuts or
filberts

½ cup blanched whole
almonds
4 eggs
1 cup light corn syrup
¾ cup sugar
1 tablespoon butter or
margarine, melted
1 teaspoon vanilla extract
¼ teaspoon salt

1. Prepare the Unbaked 9-inch Piecrust.

2. Prepare the Four-Nut Filling: Heat the oven to 350° F. Set aside 9 walnut halves, 19 pecan halves, 9 hazelnuts, and 18 almonds to garnish the top of the pie. In a food processor fitted with the chopping blade, combine the remaining nuts, the eggs, corn syrup, sugar, butter, vanilla, and salt; process until the nuts are finely chopped and the mixture is well blended.

3. Pour the nut filling into the pastry-lined plate. Starting at the outer edge of the filling, make evenly spaced, concentric circles of nuts using 16 of the reserved pecans and all the walnuts, hazelnuts, and almonds. Place the remaining 3 pecans in the center of the pie in a spoke design.

4. Bake the pie 40 to 45 minutes, or until the center is just set. Cool the pie completely on a wire rack. Refrigerate any remaining pie.

Four-Nut Pie, page 52

Pear and Cheddar Pie, page 57

Dutch Apple Pie

Cooks in Pennsylvania Dutch homes were famous for ending a meal with a dessert as hearty and satisfying as the main course. This is a high-crust, apple-packed pie. Glazed after baking, it's brought to the table glistening and golden brown.

MAKES ONE 9-INCH PIE

Pastry for a Two-Crust Pie (page 83)

Apple Filling:
9 medium-size tart cooking apples, peeled, cored, and sliced
¼ cup dark seedless raisins
1 cup granulated sugar
¼ cup all-purpose flour

½ teaspoon ground cinnamon
¼ teaspoon ground mace
⅛ teaspoon salt

Glaze:
1¼ cups confectioners' sugar
1 teaspoon lemon juice
3 to 4 teaspoons milk

1. Prepare the Pastry for a Two-Crust Pie.

2. Prepare the Apple Filling: In a large bowl, combine the apples and raisins. In a small bowl, combine the granulated sugar, flour, cinnamon, mace, and salt. Stir the sugar mixture into the apple mixture.

3. Heat the oven to 425°F. On a lightly floured surface, roll out half the pastry into an 11-inch round. Fit the pastry into a deep 9-inch pie plate. Spoon the apple filling into the pastry-lined plate. Roll out the remaining pastry into a 10-inch round. With water, moisten the rim of the pastry-lined plate. Place the pastry round on the filling. Fold the edge of the top pastry under the edge of the bottom pastry so that it is even with the rim of the plate; flute the pastry edge. Cut slits in the top crust to allow steam to escape during baking. Place the pie on a rimmed baking sheet.

4. Bake the pie 45 to 50 minutes, or until the filling bubbles in the center. Cool completely on a wire rack.

5. Prepare the Glaze: In a small bowl, combine the confectioners' sugar, lemon juice, and 3 teaspoons milk; stir until smooth. Add an additional 1 teaspoon milk, if necessary, to make the glaze a spreading consistency. Spread the glaze over the top crust of the pie and serve.

Spicy Pumpkin-Molasses Pie

Here is the dark and rich holiday dessert popular among New Englanders.

Unbaked 9-inch Piecrust
  (page 82)

Pumpkin-Molasses Filling:
3 eggs
1 16-ounce can pumpkin
  (2 cups)
1 cup milk

¼ cup sugar
½ cup light molasses
2 teaspoons ground
  cinnamon
½ teaspoon ground nutmeg
½ teaspoon ground ginger
½ teaspoon salt
1 teaspoon vanilla extract

1. Prepare the Unbaked 9-inch Piecrust.

2. Prepare the Pumpkin-Molasses Filling: Heat the oven to 400°F. Place the eggs in a large bowl. Spoon ½ teaspoon of the egg white into the piecrust. Brush the egg white over the bottom of the piecrust.

3. Stir the pumpkin, milk, sugar, molasses, cinnamon, nutmeg, ginger, salt, and vanilla into the remaining eggs until smooth. Pour the pumpkin filling into the piecrust.

4. Bake the pie 50 minutes, or until the center appears firm when the pie is gently shaken. Cool on a wire rack.

READY-MADE CRUST

You can wrap unbaked piecrusts tightly in aluminum foil and freeze them for up to 3 months. You needn't thaw before baking. Fill the pie as usual and bake in the preheated oven 5 to 10 minutes longer than the recipe directs.

Pear and Cheddar Pie
PHOTOGRAPH ON PAGE 54

A favorite European combination of sweet-ripened pear, onion, and Cheddar cheese comes together in this unusual pie filling, which is baked in a savory pastry crust. We use a rectangular tart pan but you can use a 10-inch pie plate. Serve this for afternoon tea or as an appetizer.

MAKES ONE 12- BY 8¼-INCH TART

Pastry:
1½ cups all-purpose flour
2 teaspoons dried tarragon
1 3-ounce package cream cheese
¼ cup (½ stick) butter or margarine
1 tablespoon distilled white vinegar
3 to 4 tablespoons cold water

Pear Filling:
1 tablespoon butter

3 medium-size pears, peeled, cored, cut into ¼-inch-thick slices, and each slice cut crosswise in half
¾ cup chopped green onions
½ cup half-and-half
1 egg
½ teaspoon ground black pepper
2 cups shredded Cheddar cheese

1. Prepare the Pastry: In a large bowl, combine the flour and tarragon. With a pastry blender or 2 knives, cut the cream cheese and butter into the flour mixture until the mixture resembles coarse crumbs. Stir in the vinegar and the cold water, 1 tablespoon at a time, until the pastry holds together. Shape the pastry into a ball. Wrap and refrigerate at least 30 minutes.

2. On a lightly floured surface, roll out the pastry into a 13- by 10-inch rectangle. Fit the pastry into a 12- by 8¼-inch fluted tart pan; trim the pastry even with the rim of the pan.

3. Prepare the Pear Filling: Heat the oven to 350°F. In a large skillet, melt the butter over medium heat. Add the pears and green onions; saute until the pears are browned, about 5 minutes. In a small bowl, combine the half-and-half, egg, and pepper. Arrange the cheese and the pear-onion mixture in the pastry-lined pan. Pour the egg mixture over all.

4. Bake the pie 35 to 40 minutes, or until the filling is firm. Cool on a wire rack 10 minutes before serving.

Pears in Port on Cornmeal Shortbread Crust
PHOTOGRAPH ON PAGE 17

A thick butter-rich cookie baked in the Scots' traditional round shape is the base for port-soaked pears. A North American contribution to the shortbread is the addition of cornmeal, which lends a sunny color and interesting texture to the crust. We use a pizza pan for the shortbread, but you can pat the dough into a 12-inch tart pan with a removable bottom or shape a circle on a baking sheet.

MAKES ONE 12-INCH TART

Pear Filling:
4 cups cranberry juice
  cocktail
2 cups ruby port
4 drops red food coloring
  (optional)
7 medium-size pears, peeled,
  halved, and cored
½ cup red currant jelly

Cornmeal Shortbread Crust:
1 cup all-purpose flour
1 cup yellow cornmeal
½ cup sugar
¼ teaspoon salt
1 cup (2 sticks) butter,
  softened
2 teaspoons vanilla extract

1. Prepare the Pear Filling: In a 4-quart saucepan, heat the cranberry juice, port, and food coloring, if desired, over high heat to boiling. Reduce the heat and add the pears. Cover and cook over low heat 10 to 15 minutes, or until the pears are just tender. Remove from the heat, and let stand 30 minutes to intensify the color.

2. Prepare the Cornmeal Shortbread Crust: In a medium-size bowl, combine the flour, cornmeal, sugar, and salt. With a pastry blender or 2 knives, cut in the butter and vanilla until a stiff dough forms.

3. Heat the oven to 375°F. Grease a 12-inch pizza pan. With floured fingers, pat the dough out to cover the bottom of the pan evenly; form a ridge at the edge of the pan.

4. With a slotted spoon, remove the pears from the port mixture. Reserve the port mixture. Arrange the pears, cut sides down, on the dough-lined pan. (If all the pear halves will not fit, cut the remaining halves into ½-inch cubes and tuck under the pear halves to fill the hollow where the core was removed, or refrigerate for another use.)

5. Score the tops of the pears several times. Bake the pear-topped shortbread 45 to 50 minutes, or until the shortbread is firm and lightly browned. Cool completely on a wire rack.

6. Meanwhile, add the currant jelly to the port mixture, and cook over low heat until the mixture is reduced to 1 cup. Drizzle the port mixture over the pears. Cut the shortbread into 10 wedges, and serve at room temperature.

Pecan Pie

....

A s they would say in the South, this is just pecan pie. It is a light golden caramel color which is popular in Georgia. For a darker pie, substitute dark brown sugar and dark syrup. And for a New England touch, replace the corn syrup with maple syrup.

MAKES ONE 9-INCH PIE

Unbaked 9-inch Piecrust
  (page 82)

Pecan Filling:
4 eggs, lightly beaten
½ cup granulated sugar
½ cup firmly packed
  light-brown sugar
1 cup light corn syrup

1 tablespoon all-purpose
  flour
1 teaspoon vanilla extract
¼ teaspoon salt
¼ cup (½ stick) butter,
  melted
1½ cups chopped pecans
1 cup pecan halves

1. Prepare the Unbaked 9-inch Piecrust.

2. Prepare the Pecan Filling: Heat the oven to 350°F. In a medium-size bowl, beat the eggs, granulated sugar, brown sugar, corn syrup, flour, vanilla, and salt until well combined. Stir in the butter and chopped pecans. Pour the pecan filling into the piecrust. Arrange the pecan halves in concentric circles on the filling.

3. Bake the pie 55 to 60 minutes, or until the filling stays firm when the pie is gently shaken. Cool on a wire rack.

Lemon Meringue Pie

Making its appearance every day on dessert menus in nearly every diner and lunch counter across the country, this translucent pie seems to be in demand and in good taste anywhere, any time. Ours is particularly lemony.

MAKES ONE 9-INCH PIE

Baked 9-inch Piecrust
(page 82)

Lemon Filling:
1 cup sugar
⅓ cup cornstarch
¼ teaspoon salt
½ cup lemon juice
⅓ cup cold water
3 egg yolks (reserve the egg
    whites for the meringue)

1 tablespoon butter or
    margarine
1½ cups boiling water
1½ teaspoons grated
    lemon rind

Meringue:
3 egg whites, at room
    temperature
¼ teaspoon cream of tartar
⅓ cup sugar

1. Prepare the Baked 9-inch Piecrust.

2. Prepare the Lemon Filling: In a 2-quart saucepan, combine the sugar, cornstarch, and salt. Stir in the lemon juice and cold water.

3. In a medium bowl, beat the egg yolks. Slowly beat the lemon mixture into the egg yolks; pour the mixture back into the saucepan. Stir in the butter and boiling water.

4. Heat the lemon mixture to boiling over medium-high heat, stirring constantly. Reduce the heat to medium, and boil just 1 minute. Stir in the lemon rind. Pour the lemon filling into the piecrust.

5. Prepare the Meringue: Heat the oven to 350° F. In a medium-size bowl, with an electric mixer on high speed, beat the egg whites and cream of tartar until soft peaks form. Gradually add the sugar, beating until stiff peaks form. Spread the meringue over the lemon filling, swirling the top and sealing to the edge of the crust.

6. Bake the pie 10 to 12 minutes, or until the meringue is golden brown. Cool on a wire rack.

Mississippi Mud Pie

....

This is not the traditional dense, fudge-like pie and crust. Instead it's an easy ice cream pie, cut into wedges and deluged with warm mocha-fudge syrup and whipped cream, then sprinkled with shaved chocolate. The chocolate crust and ice cream filling can be assembled one day ahead.

MAKES ONE 9-INCH PIE

Chocolate Crust:
¼ cup butter or margarine
2 cups chocolate wafer
   crumbs (36 wafers)

Ice Cream Filling:
2 pints coffee ice cream
1 pint chocolate or chocolate
   chip ice cream

Mocha-Fudge Syrup:
6 1-ounce squares semisweet
   chocolate
3 tablespoons light corn syrup
¼ cup coffee-flavored liqueur

2 cups Sweetened Whipped
   Cream (page 13)
1 1-ounce square unsweet-
   ened chocolate, shaved

1. Prepare the Chocolate Crust: Heat the oven to 350°F. In a small saucepan, melt the butter over low heat. Remove from the heat and stir in the chocolate crumbs. Press the crumb mixture firmly into the bottom and side of a 9-inch pie plate, making a raised edge about ⅛-inch around the rim of the pie plate. Bake the crust 8 minutes. Cool completely on a wire rack.

2. Prepare the Ice Cream Filling: Soften the ice cream at room temperature for 15 minutes. Spoon the ice cream into the pie plate, alternating the 2 flavors to marbleize. Cover the pie with plastic wrap, and freeze until firm, about 2 hours.

3. Prepare the Mocha-Fudge Syrup: Just before serving, in a small saucepan, combine the chocolate and corn syrup. Cook over medium heat, stirring constantly, until the chocolate melts. Stir in the liqueur. Remove from heat.

4. To serve, cut the pie into wedges. Top each wedge with syrup, sweetened whipped cream, and shaved chocolate.

Raisin Pie

....

Here is an old-fashioned American breakfast pie, which was served to farmhands when breakfast was a major meal and included dessert. It has since become a staple dessert in many Midwestern restaurants and roadside diners.

MAKES ONE 10-INCH PIE

Pastry for a One-Crust Pie (page 82)

Raisin Filling:
4 cups water
4 cups dark seedless raisins
1 cup sugar
⅓ cup all-purpose flour

½ teaspoon ground cinnamon
¼ teaspoon ground nutmeg
1 teaspoon grated lemon rind
2 tablespoons lemon juice

Sour cream or whipped cream (optional)
Walnut halves (optional)

1. Prepare the Pastry for a One-Crust Pie.
2. Prepare the Raisin Filling: In a 3-quart saucepan, heat the water to boiling over high heat. Add the raisins; return to boiling. Reduce the heat to low; cover and simmer until the raisins are plump and tender, about 8 minutes. Meanwhile, in a small bowl, combine the sugar, flour, cinnamon, and nutmeg.
3. Stir the sugar mixture into the raisins; cook over medium heat, stirring constantly, until the mixture comes to a boil. Remove from the heat; stir in the lemon rind and lemon juice. Let stand until cool.
4. Heat the oven to 425°F. On a lightly floured surface, roll out the pastry into a 13-inch round. Fit the pastry into a 10-inch pie plate. Fold the pastry overhang under so that it is even with the rim of the plate; flute the pastry edge. Line the pastry with aluminum foil and add uncooked dried beans or pie weights.
5. Bake the pastry 8 to 10 minutes, or just until firm. Remove the beans and foil. Bake the pastry 8 to 10 minutes longer, or until lightly brown. Cool the piecrust completely on a wire rack. Spoon the raisin filling into the piecrust. Refrigerate the pie until well chilled, several hours or overnight. Just before serving, top the pie with sour cream or whipped cream and walnuts, if desired.

Shoofly Pie

....

We recommend a dark molasses, which is a little less sweet than light molasses, for this traditional Pennsylvania Dutch pie. Food lore has it that the dessert got its name because it was so sweet that at outdoor meals it lured the flies away from the main table.

MAKES ONE 9-INCH PIE

Unbaked 9-inch Piecrust
  (page 82)

Molasses Filling:
1½ cups all-purpose flour
½ cup firmly packed
  light-brown sugar

2 tablespoons butter, softened
1¼ cups dark molasses
1 egg
1 cup very hot water (145° -
  155°F)
1 teaspoon baking soda

1. Prepare the Unbaked 9-inch Piecrust.

2. Prepare the Molasses Filling: Heat the oven to 350°F. In a medium-size bowl, combine the flour and brown sugar. With a pastry blender or 2 knives, cut the butter into the flour mixture until the mixture resembles coarse crumbs.

3. In a medium-size bowl, combine the molasses, egg, and ¾ cup very hot water. Stir the baking soda into the remaining ¼ cup very hot water and immediately stir into the molasses mixture.

4. Pour half the molasses mixture into the piecrust. Sprinkle with half of the crumb mixture. Pour all but ¼ cup of the remaining molasses mixture over the crumb mixture. Sprinkle with the remaining crumb mixture. Drizzle the reserved ¼ cup molasses mixture in a spiral over the top of the pie.

5. Bake the pie 40 to 45 minutes, or until the center appears firm when the pie is gently shaken. Cool completely on a wire rack.

> NATIONAL PIE DAY IS JANUARY 23!

Southern Lime Pie

....

Fresh limes are available year round but they are truly at their tangy best May through August. Buy bright, smooth-skinned limes that feel heavier than they look. If you are lucky enough to find key limes, usually available only in Florida, by all means use them. Bottled key lime juice is also fine in this recipe.

Makes one 9-inch pie

Baked 9-inch Piecrust (page 82)	*½ cup fresh lime juice*
	¼ teaspoon salt
	Few drops green food coloring
Lime Filling:	
1 14-ounce can sweetened condensed milk (not evaporated milk)	*½ cup shredded or flaked coconut*
¼ teaspoon grated lime rind	*1 cup (½ pint) heavy cream*

1. Prepare the Baked 9-inch Piecrust.

2. Prepare the Lime Filling: In a large bowl, combine the condensed milk, lime rind, lime juice, salt, and food coloring; stir until well blended. Refrigerate until cold and thickened.

3. Sprinkle the coconut on the bottom of the piecrust. Pour the chilled lime mixture into the crust. In a small bowl, with an electric mixer on medium speed, beat the cream until stiff peaks form. Spread the whipped cream over the pie, sealing to the edge. Refrigerate the pie 6 to 8 hours before serving.

STORE-BOUGHT PUFF PASTRY

Ready-made frozen puff pastry is a boon because it is so work-intensive to make at home. It keeps for several months. Let it thaw slowly, tightly covered to prevent drying out, in the refrigerator 8 hours or overnight. Once thawed, use it to top savory pies or to create delicate lattice tops.

Dorothy Lamb's Peanut Butter Pie

PHOTOGRAPH ON PAGE 71

Ordinary peanut butter — not the expensive health-food store variety — is best to use because of its light melting qualities.

MAKES ONE 9-INCH PIE

Baked 9-inch Piecrust
(page 82)

Peanut Butter Filling:
¾ cup confectioners' sugar
½ cup creamy peanut butter
¾ cup granulated sugar
3 tablespoons cornstarch
1 tablespoon all-purpose
flour
⅛ teaspoon salt

3 egg yolks (reserve the whites
for the meringue)
3 cups milk
2 teaspoons butter or
margarine
2 teaspoons vanilla extract

Meringue Topping:
3 egg whites, at room
temperature
¼ teaspoon cream of tartar

1. Prepare the Baked 9-inch Piecrust.

2. Prepare the Peanut Butter Filling: Place the confectioners' sugar in a small bowl. With a fork, cut the peanut butter into the sugar until the mixture resembles coarse crumbs.

3. In a 2-quart saucepan, combine ½ cup granulated sugar, the cornstarch, flour, and salt. With a wire whisk, stir the egg yolks and milk into the granulated sugar mixture. Heat to boiling and cook, stirring constantly, 2 minutes. Remove the pudding from the heat; stir in the butter and vanilla. Sprinkle one third of the peanut crumbs over the bottom of the piecrust. Spoon half the pudding over the crumbs. Sprinkle with another third of the crumbs, and top with the remaining pudding.

4. Prepare the Meringue Topping: Heat the oven to 375°F. In a medium-size bowl, with an electric mixer on high speed, beat the egg whites and the cream of tartar until soft peaks form. Gradually sprinkle the remaining ¼ cup granulated sugar over the egg whites. Beat until stiff peaks form. Spread the meringue over the pudding, sealing to the edge of the crust. With a spatula, swirl the top of the meringue. Sprinkle the remaining third of the peanut butter crumbs around edge.

5. Bake the pie 10 to 12 minutes, or until the meringue is golden brown. Cool on a wire rack.

Cherry Crumb Pie

....

A quick pie to satisfy a sudden craving, this uses canned cherries. Hints of nutmeg and cinnamon give a slight autumnal flavor to one of our most popular summer fruits.

MAKES ONE 9-INCH PIE

Unbaked 9-inch Piecrust
(page 82)

Cherry Filling:
⅓ cup granulated sugar
2 tablespoons cornstarch
2 16-ounce cans pitted sour
cherries, drained, liquid
reserved
1 tablespoon lemon juice
½ teaspoon almond extract

Crumb Topping:
¾ cup all-purpose flour
⅓ cup firmly packed
light-brown sugar
¼ teaspoon ground
cinnamon
Pinch of salt
¼ cup (½ stick) butter or
margarine, melted
¼ teaspoon almond extract

1. Prepare the Unbaked 9-inch Piecrust.

2. Prepare the Cherry Filling: Heat the oven to 350°F. In a 2-quart saucepan, mix the granulated sugar, cornstarch, 1 cup of the reserved cherry liquid, and the lemon juice. Heat to boiling over medium heat, stirring constantly. Cook until thickened, about 6 minutes. Remove from the heat and fold in the cherries and almond extract.

3. Prepare the Crumb Topping: In a small bowl, combine the flour, brown sugar, cinnamon, and salt. With a fork, stir in the butter and almond extract until the mixture resembles coarse crumbs.

4. Spoon the cherry filling into the prepared piecrust. Sprinkle evenly with the crumb topping. Place the pie on a rimmed baking sheet.

5. Bake the pie 40 to 45 minutes, or until the filling bubbles in the center. Cool completely on a wire rack before serving.

Apple Pie

....

The secret to good apple pie is beginning with good apples and then having plenty of them to mound up in the pie plate so that your pie is high and ample looking. We suggest our favorite Granny Smith apple here and if 6 cups isn't enough to pile high in your pie plate, increase the apples to 9 cups and add another ¼ cup sugar.

MAKES ONE 9-INCH PIE

Pastry for a Two-Crust Pie
  (page 83)

Apple Filling:
1 cup plus 1 teaspoon sugar
2 tablespoons all-purpose
  flour
1 teaspoon ground cinnamon

½ teaspoon ground nutmeg
4 large Granny Smith apples,
  peeled, cored, and sliced
2 tablespoons butter or
  margarine, cut into pieces

1 tablespoon milk (optional)

1. Prepare the Pastry for a Two-Crust Pie: Heat the oven to 425°F. On a lightly floured surface, roll out half the pastry into an 11-inch round. Fit the pastry into a 9-inch pie plate, leaving the edge untrimmed.

2. Prepare the Apple Filling: In a small bowl, combine 1 cup sugar, the flour, cinnamon, and nutmeg. Place half the apple slices in the pastry-lined plate. Sprinkle with half the sugar mixture. Repeat with the remaining apple slices and sugar mixture. Dot with the butter.

3. Roll out the remaining pastry into a 10-inch round. With water, moisten the rim of the pastry-lined plate. Place the pastry round on the filling. Fold the edge of the top pastry under the edge of the bottom pastry so that it is even with the rim of the plate; flute the pastry edge. If desired, brush the pie with the milk and sprinkle with 1 teaspoon sugar. With a fork, pierce the top to allow steam to escape during baking.

4. Bake the pie 40 to 45 minutes, or until the filling bubbles in the center. Cool on a wire rack.

Hearty Rancher's Pie

....

A wintertime one-pot meal of beef and chili, carrots, corn, and peppers stewed together, then baked under a blanket of creamy potatoes and jack cheese, this is a Texas version of England's Shepherd's Pie.

MAKES 8 SERVINGS

½ cup dried red kidney beans
¼ cup all-purpose flour
1 teaspoon salt
⅛ teaspoon ground black
   pepper
1½ pounds lean beef chuck,
   cut into 1-inch cubes
1 tablespoon olive oil
1 large onion, sliced
2 cloves garlic, finely
   chopped
1 12-ounce can beer
2 medium-size carrots,
   peeled and sliced
2 teaspoons chili powder
1 teaspoon ground cumin

1½ pounds all-purpose
   potatoes
¼ cup half-and-half
1 egg
1 10-ounce package frozen
   whole-kernel corn, thawed
1 medium-size sweet red
   pepper, coarsely chopped
1 medium-size sweet green
   pepper, coarsely chopped
1 6-ounce can vegetable juice
   cocktail
½ cup shredded Monterey
   Jack cheese

1. In a 2-quart saucepan, combine the beans and enough water to cover. Heat to boiling over high heat. Reduce the heat to low and simmer 2 minutes; remove the beans from the heat. Let stand, covered, for 1 hour. Drain the beans, reserving the liquid. Add water to the reserved liquid to make 1 cup.

2. In a plastic bag, combine the flour, ½ teaspoon salt, and the pepper. Add the beef cubes, one half at a time, and shake to coat with the flour mixture. Reserve the remaining flour mixture.

3. In a heavy 4-quart saucepan, heat the oil over medium-high heat. Saute the beef cubes, one half at a time, until browned on all sides, about 5 minutes. Remove the beef cubes to a plate or baking pan as they are browned. Add the onion and garlic to the pan; saute until golden.

4. Return the beef and its juices to the saucepan with the onion. Add the beer, carrots, chili powder, cumin, and remaining ½ teaspoon salt. Stir in the beans and the reserved 1 cup liquid. Heat the mixture to boiling over medium heat; reduce the heat to low and cook, covered, 1¼ to 1½ hours, or until the beef is tender. Add water if the mixture becomes dry.

5. Meanwhile, peel and quarter the potatoes. In a 3-quart saucepan, cook the potatoes in boiling water until tender, about 20 minutes.

6. Meanwhile, in a small saucepan, heat the half-and-half over low heat just until warm. Drain the potatoes very well; return to the saucepan. With a portable or hand-held electric mixer on medium speed, beat the potatoes until well broken up. Gradually beat in the half-and-half and egg until the potato mixture is smooth; keep warm.

7. When the beef is tender, add the corn and peppers; cover and cook 10 minutes longer. In a small bowl, combine the reserved flour mixture and the vegetable juice cocktail, and stir into the stew. Cook, stirring constantly, until thickened.

8. Heat the oven to 425°F. Spoon the beef mixture into a shallow 3-quart baking dish. Spoon the potatoes over the top of the beef. Sprinkle with the shredded cheese. Bake the pie until the cheese is melted. Serve immediately.

BAKING IN QUANTITY

A 9-inch pie or tart will serve 8 to 10 and a 10-inch tart will serve 10 to 12 or more, depending on the richness of the tart and the generosity of the server.

Most of our recipes for dessert pies and tarts can be doubled. Fruit pies especially are often doubled, even tripled during seasons of abundant fruit harvests. But don't crowd pies in the oven. When baking more than one at a time, be sure to leave at least 1½ inches of space between the oven wall and the next pie.

Vegetarian Cornish Pasty

....

For the no-meat pasty lover this is every bit as satisfying as the meaty Cornish variety (page 73). You can safely double this recipe to make four pasties.

MAKES TWO 9- BY 4½-INCH PASTIES

Country Pastry:
3 cups all-purpose flour
1 teaspoon salt
1 cup vegetable shortening
6 to 7 tablespoons cold water

Vegetable Filling:
2 large potatoes, peeled and
*   diced*

1 large onion, chopped
2 carrots, peeled and sliced
1 large turnip, peeled and
*   chopped*
Salt and pepper
2 tablespoons butter, cut into
*   tiny pieces*

1. Prepare the Pastry: In a medium-size bowl, mix the flour and salt. With a pastry blender or 2 knives, cut the shortening into the flour mixture until the mixture resembles coarse crumbs. Stir in the cold water, 1 tablespoon at a time, just until the mixture holds together. Divide the pastry into 2 equal-size balls. Wrap and refrigerate at least 30 minutes. On a lightly floured surface, roll out each pastry half into a 9-inch round. Place each round on an ungreased baking sheet.

2. Prepare the Vegetable Filling: Heat the oven to 350°F. In a large bowl, mix the potatoes, onion, carrots, and turnip. Add salt and pepper to taste. Spoon half the vegetable filling onto half of each pastry round. Dot each round with 1 tablespoon butter. Fold the pastry over the top of the filling. Press the edges together and flute. With a fork, pierce the top to allow steam to escape during baking.

3. Bake the pasties 1 hour, or until golden brown. Serve warm or at room temperature.

Dorothy Lamb's Peanut Butter Pie, page 65

Red, White, and Blue Pie, page 22

Cornish Pasty

....

These are the savory meat-filled turnovers named after the 18th- and 19th-Century coal miners from Cornwall, England, who devoured them daily for lunch. Some pasties were very large — one half rolled around meat and the other half filled with apple for dessert.

MAKES EIGHT 9- BY 4½-INCH PASTIES

Country Pastry:
1 cup vegetable shortening
1¼ cups boiling water
1 teaspoon salt
4½ to 5 cups all-purpose
* flour*

Beef-Vegetable Filling:
1¾ pounds boneless beef
* sirloin or top round steak,*
* cut into ¼-inch cubes*

4 medium-size potatoes,
* peeled and diced*
1 large onion, finely chopped
1 cup finely chopped peeled
* rutabaga*
1 cup sliced carrots
1 teaspoon salt
½ teaspoon ground black
* pepper*

1. Prepare the Country Pastry: Place the shortening in a large bowl; add the boiling water and stir until the shortening melts. Stir in the salt and enough of the flour to form a stiff dough. Shape the pastry into a ball; wrap in plastic wrap, and refrigerate at least 1 hour.

2. Prepare the Beef-Vegetable Filling: In a large bowl, combine the beef, potatoes, onion, rutabaga, carrots, salt, and pepper.

3. Divide the pastry into 8 pieces. On a lightly floured surface, roll out one piece of the pastry into a 9-inch round. Place the round on an ungreased baking sheet. Spoon one eighth (about 1 cup) of the beef mixture onto the center of the round. Lift 2 opposite sides of the round over the filling. Pinch the sides firmly together to seal from the center to the 2 pointed ends that form. Fold the edge over to form a double-thick, ½-inch-wide seam. Crimp the seam with fingers to form a decorative rope. Repeat to make 8 pasties in all. With a fork, pierce the top of each to allow steam to escape during baking.

4. Heat the oven to 350°F. Bake the pasties 1 to 1¼ hours or until golden. Serve the pasties warm or at room temperature.

Aberdeen Beef Pie

....

This is a hearty combination of beef and vegetables, slowly stewed in dark ale and seasonings, and topped with a delicate puff-pastry crust.

MAKES 6 SERVINGS

8 ounces (½ package) frozen
  puff pastry
½ teaspoon vegetable oil
¼ pound lean bacon,
  chopped
3 pounds beef round, cubed
1 cup whole pearl onions,
  peeled
½ pound baby carrots, peeled
  and trimmed
1 teaspoon dried thyme leaves

1 14½- or 13¾-ounce can
  beef broth
½ cup dark beer
2 tablespoons all-purpose
  flour
1 tablespoon Worcestershire
  sauce
½ cup frozen green peas,
  thawed (optional)
1 egg
2 teaspoons water

1. Thaw the puff pastry overnight in the refrigerator or according to the package directions. In an ovenproof 5-quart Dutch oven, heat the oil. Add the bacon and saute until lightly browned, about 4 minutes. Add the beef and brown on all sides. Remove the beef and bacon to a plate. Add the onions to the Dutch oven and saute until lightly browned, about 8 minutes. Add the beef, bacon, carrots, and thyme to the Dutch oven. Remove from heat.

2. Heat the oven to 350°F. In a medium-size bowl, with a wire whisk, beat the broth, beer, flour, and Worcestershire sauce until smooth; stir into the beef mixture in the Dutch oven. Heat the mixture to boiling over medium heat. Remove from the heat. Cover and bake 1 hour, or until the beef is tender. If desired, stir in the peas. Spoon the beef mixture into a 2-quart casserole or baking dish. Set aside.

3. Heat the oven to 400°F. On a lightly floured surface, roll out a sheet of puff pastry into a 16- by 14-inch rectangle. Cut 2 lengthwise ½-inch-wide strips from the pastry; set aside. Cut the remaining rolled-out puff pastry, crosswise, into ½-inch-wide strips. On lightly floured waxed paper, crisscross the strips to form a basket weave. Invert the woven strips onto the top of the casserole; remove the waxed paper. Trim the ends to the rim. With the palm of the hand, roll the reserved

Mustard-Onion Pie

strips to make two 25-inch ropes. Twist the ropes together, and pinch the ends to form one braided rope. In a small bowl, combine the egg and water. Brush the rim of the casserole with some of the egg mixture. Press the braided rope around the rim. Brush the egg mixture over the rope and basket weave pastry.

4. Bake the casserole 15 to 20 minutes, or until the crust is golden brown. Serve immediately.

A n excellent savory to serve as an appetizer, or with a salad for a light lunch, this is a creamy cheese and onion combination.

MAKES ONE 9-INCH PIE

Unbaked 9-inch Piecrust
(page 82)

Mustard-Onion Filling:
1 tablespoon butter or
olive oil
1½ pounds onions, sliced
1 8-ounce container plain
yogurt

1 4-ounce package French
triple-crème cheese
with pepper
2 eggs
2 tablespoons Dijon-style
prepared mustard
2 cups shredded Gruyère
cheese

1. Prepare the Unbaked 9-inch Piecrust.
2. Prepare the Mustard-Onion Filling: Heat the oven to 350°F. In a large skillet, melt the butter over medium heat. Add the onions, and saute, stirring occasionally, until golden, 5 to 7 minutes.
3. In a medium-size bowl, with an electric mixer on medium speed, beat the yogurt, triple-crème cheese, eggs, and mustard until smooth. Spoon the onions into the piecrust. Top with the cheese mixture. Sprinkle the shredded Gruyère cheese over the top.
4. Bake the pie 40 to 45 minutes, or until the filling is set and golden brown. Cool 10 minutes on a wire rack before serving.

Shepherd's Pie

Here is a hearty deep-dish pie as welcome at the table in the big sheep country of Wyoming as it has been for the past two centuries in the British Isles. Full of lamb and vegetables, it's topped with fluffy mashed potatoes and baked until the potatoes turn golden brown.

MAKES 6 SERVINGS

¼ all-purpose flour
¾ teaspoon salt
⅛ teaspoon ground black pepper
1½ pounds lean, boneless lamb shoulder, cut into 1-inch cubes
1 tablespoon olive or vegetable oil
¼ pound mushrooms, sliced
1 large onion, sliced
2 cloves garlic, finely chopped
1 12-ounce can ale or beer

2 medium-size carrots, peeled and sliced
¼ teaspoon dried rosemary, crumbled
1½ pounds all-purpose potatoes
¼ cup half-and-half, warmed
1 egg
½ cup shredded white Cheddar cheese
1 10-ounce package frozen green peas, thawed
¼ cup water

1. In a plastic bag, combine the flour, salt, and pepper. Add the lamb cubes, one half at a time, and shake to coat with the flour mixture. Reserve the remaining flour mixture.

2. In a heavy 4-quart saucepan or Dutch oven, heat the oil. Saute the lamb cubes, one half at a time, until browned on all sides. Remove the cubes to a plate or baking pan as they are browned. Add the mushrooms, onion, and garlic; saute until golden.

3. Return the lamb and its juices to the saucepan. Add the ale, carrots, and rosemary. Heat the mixture to boiling over medium heat; reduce the heat to low and cook, covered, about 30 minutes, adding more water if the mixture becomes dry.

4. Meanwhile, peel and quarter the potatoes. In a 3-quart saucepan, cook the potatoes in boiling water until tender, about 20 minutes.

5. Drain the potatoes very well; return to the saucepan. With a portable or hand-held electric mixer on medium speed, beat the potatoes until well broken up. Gradually beat in the half-and-half and

egg until the potato mixture is smooth. Fold in the cheese; keep warm.

6. When the lamb has cooked about 30 minutes, add the peas; cover and cook 10 minutes longer. In a small bowl, combine the reserved flour mixture and ¼ cup water and stir into the stew. Cook, stirring constantly, until thickened.

7. Heat the oven to 425°F. Spoon the lamb mixture into a shallow 2-quart baking dish. Spoon the potatoes into a large pastry bag fitted with a large star tip. Pipe the potatoes to cover the top of the lamb mixture. Bake the pie 15 to 20 minutes, or until the potatoes are browned.

PERFECT PASTRY

To ensure a tender-crisp, flaky crust, mix the dough carefully, patiently cutting the butter or fat into the flour until every tiny, crumb-like morsel is coated with flour. Be watchful during this process. Keep the mixture dry and stop when it resembles coarse crumbs, before it becomes fine crumbs. If it becomes thick or oily, you have over-mixed. It is those tiny, lightly flour-covered fatty crumbs that puff up during baking and create the flaky layers in the pastry.

For the same reason, pastry dough should be handled as little as possible. As you manipulate the dough, the flour and butter or shortening become more and more kneaded together and the dough develops an elasticity that makes it tough. To create a soft dough, stir water a little at a time into the coarse crumb mixture. The mixture will slowly progress from a lumpy mix to a soft dough. If the dough can hold together when you press it into a ball, it's ready. If it seems dry, add more water, a few drops at a time. The amount of water will depend on the absorbency of the flour.

If the dough is intended for a two-crust pie, divide it in half and shape each half into a ball or a 1-inch-thick disk. Wrap them in plastic wrap and refrigerate for 30 minutes to 1 hour to let the dough rest. During this rest period it will become more manageable and easier to roll out.

Spinach and Tofu Quiche

....

Tofu, a high-protein soybean cake, and tahini, a light creamy sauce made from sesame seeds, are two ingredients in this quiche that can be found at Asian-American markets and health-food stores. This is a dairy-free vegetarian quiche that is extremely flavorful and satisfying. The whole-wheat crust is not as tender as most but is full of nutty flavor.

MAKES ONE 9-INCH QUICHE

Whole-Wheat Crust:
1 cup all-purpose flour
½ cup whole-wheat flour
½ teaspoon salt
⅓ cup canola or light olive oil
3 tablespoons cold water

Spinach-Tofu Filling:
1 pound spinach leaves (12 cups loosely packed), or 2 10-ounce packages frozen spinach, thawed and well drained
1 tablespoon sesame oil
2 cloves garlic, chopped
1 medium-size onion, chopped

1 teaspoon Worcestershire sauce
1 tablespoon cornstarch
3 tablespoons water
1 10-ounce container soft tofu, drained
2 tablespoons tahini (see Note)
½ teaspoon salt
¼ teaspoon ground black pepper
⅛ teaspoon ground nutmeg
1 teaspoon sesame seeds, toasted
Red pepper strips for garnish (optional)

1. Prepare the Whole-Wheat Crust: Heat the oven to 400°F. In a large bowl, combine the all-purpose flour, whole-wheat flour, and salt. Stir in the oil and the cold water, 1 tablespoon at a time, until the mixture holds together. Shape pastry into a ball.

2. On lightly floured waxed paper, roll out the pastry into a 10-inch round. Fit the pastry into a 9-inch pie plate. Trim the pastry even with the rim of the pie plate. With a fork, flute the pastry edge. Line the pastry with aluminum foil and fill with uncooked dried beans or pie weights. Bake the pastry 10 minutes; remove the beans and foil. Cool the piecrust in the pan on a wire rack.

3. Prepare the Spinach-Tofu Filling: If using fresh spinach, remove the tough stems from the leaves. In a 5-quart Dutch oven, heat the oil. Add the garlic and onion; saute until the onion is transparent, about 3 minutes. Add the Worcestershire sauce and spinach; cover and cook 2 minutes. Stir the spinach and cook, covered, 2 minutes longer. In a small bowl, combine the cornstarch and water; stir into the spinach mixture. Remove the pan from the heat. Cool the spinach mixture slightly. In a food processor fitted with the chopping blade, process the spinach mixture until coarsely chopped.

4. Reduce the oven temperature to 375°F. In a medium-size bowl, combine the spinach mixture, tofu, tahini, salt, pepper, and nutmeg; pour the mixture into the piecrust. Bake the quiche 30 minutes, or until the top is golden brown. Sprinkle the top with sesame seeds, and garnish with red pepper strips, if desired. Serve the quiche immediately.

PERFECT CRUST

Roll out the dough on a surface that offers the least resistance possible. We suggest a floured board, but a countertop, a cool marble slab, or a pastry cloth all are good choices. A rolling pin fitted with a stockinette works well, too.

Sprinkle the disk of dough with flour and dust the rolling pin with flour. Beginning in the center, roll the dough into a 12-inch circle of even thickness. Roll in all directions about 2-inches at a time, pushing the dough again and again into a circular shape. Don't roll over the edge because it tends to thin out.

If you're using waxed paper with tender pastry, simply turn the paper base a quarter turn after every few rolls until you have a circle of dough large enough to fit into a pie plate. To fit the dough into the pie plate, invert the waxed paper with the pastry over the pie plate and gently peel away the paper. Press the dough to fit snugly into the plate and leave the overhang untrimmed.

Chicken Pie

....

In the New England tradition, these individual casseroles topped with golden pastry make single-serving whole meals and are best served with a green salad on the side and a light dessert. To make one large pie instead, use a 2- to 2½-quart casserole and top with pastry.

MAKES 6 INDIVIDUAL PIES

Pastry for a Two-Crust Pie (page 83)

Chicken Filling:
1 3-pound chicken, cut into pieces
2 cups water
1 teaspoon salt
½ teaspoon dried basil
⅛ teaspoon ground black pepper
1 pound all-purpose potatoes, peeled and cut into 1-inch chunks

½ pound carrots, peeled and sliced
1 stalk celery, sliced
1 tablespoon butter or margarine
¼ pound small fresh mushrooms, quartered
1 cup coarsely chopped onions
1 cup frozen green peas, thawed
½ cup all-purpose flour

1. Prepare the Pastry for a Two-Crust Pie.

2. Prepare the Chicken Filling: Rinse and drain the chicken, neck, and giblets. In a 4-quart saucepan or Dutch oven, combine the chicken, neck, giblets, 1½ cups water, the salt, basil, and pepper. Heat to boiling over high heat. Reduce the heat to low and simmer, covered, until the chicken is tender, about 45 minutes.

3. With a slotted spoon, remove the chicken and giblets to a medium-size bowl; set aside to cool slightly. Discard the neck. Add the potatoes, carrots, and celery to the simmering broth. Cook until the vegetables are tender, about 15 minutes. Meanwhile, in a small skillet, melt the butter. Add the mushrooms and saute until golden brown, about 5 minutes. Stir in the onions and peas; set aside.

4. Remove the skin and bones from the chicken; discard. Cut the chicken into 1- to 1½-inch pieces. In a large bowl, combine the chicken

and the mushroom mixture. With a slotted spoon, remove the vegetables from the broth; drain well and add to the chicken mixture.

5. Strain the chicken broth into a 1-quart measuring cup. Return 2 cups broth to the saucepan. In a small bowl, stir the remaining ½ cup water into the flour. Stir the mixture into the broth in the saucepan. Heat to boiling, stirring constantly until thickened. Remove from the heat.

6. Heat the oven to 375°F. Lightly grease six 1½-cup individual serving casseroles or gratin dishes. Spoon the chicken and the vegetables into the casseroles, and divide the thickened broth among them. Divide each half of the pastry into 3 pieces. On a lightly floured surface, roll out each piece of pastry into a round large enough to fit over one casserole, and place them over the casseroles. Fold each pastry overhang under so that it is even with the rim of the casserole; flute the pastry edge. With a fork, pierce the tops to allow steam to escape during baking. Place the casseroles on a rimmed baking sheet.

7. Bake the casseroles 40 to 45 minutes, or until the filling bubbles in the center. Serve immediately.

SAVE THOSE PASTRY SCRAPS

R e-rolled and cut with any number of different-shaped cookie cutters, pastry cutouts can be baked at 350°F for 10 minutes, dusted with cinnamon sugar or vanilla sugar, and served with afternoon tea or a glass of cold milk.

Pastry cutouts can decorate the top crust or border of any two-crust sweet or savory pie. Use a leaf cookie cutter or template, for example, to cut out a few leaf shapes from re-rolled dough. With a sharp knife, score lines to resemble veins. Use a pastry brush to moisten the bottom sides of the pastry leaves with water and press onto the top crust just before baking.

For border decorations on an open-face pie, gently crimp but do not flute the edge. Instead, apply a border of pastry cutouts such as small stars or flowers all around the edge of the pie before baking.

Pastry Crusts

....

A tender, flaky crust begins with a handmade pastry dough. If you try to make this in a processor or blender without the help of your own hands to tell you how dry or moist the pastry is, you may end up with an over-blended dough and a tough crust.

Pastry for a One-Crust Pie

....

MAKES PASTRY FOR ONE 9-INCH PIE

1⅓ cups all-purpose flour
¼ teaspoon salt
6 tablespoons (¾ stick)
   butter or margarine

2 tablespoons vegetable
   shortening
2 to 3 tablespoons cold water

1. In a medium-size bowl, combine the flour and salt. With a pastry blender or 2 knives, cut the butter and shortening into the flour mixture until the mixture resembles coarse crumbs.

2. Sprinkle the cold water over the flour mixture, 1 tablespoon at a time, and mix lightly until the pastry holds together when lightly pressed. Shape the pastry into a ball; flatten to a 1-inch thickness. Wrap and refrigerate the pastry at least 30 minutes.

Unbaked 9-inch Piecrust

On a lightly floured surface, roll out the pastry into an 11-inch round. Fit the pastry into a 9-inch pie plate. Fold the pastry overhang under so that it is even with the rim of the plate, and flute the pastry edge.

Baked 9-inch Piecrust

Heat the oven to 425°F. Prepare the pastry and fit into the pie plate as directed above. With a fork, pierce the bottom and side of the pastry to prevent shrinkage. Line the pastry with aluminium foil and fill with uncooked dried beans or pie weights. Bake the pastry 15 minutes. Remove the beans and foil and bake 5 to 10 minutes, or until the crust is golden. Cool the piecrust completely on a wire rack.

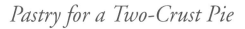

Pastry for a Two-Crust Pie

....

MAKES PASTRY FOR ONE 9-INCH TWO-CRUST PIE

2 cups all-purpose flour
½ teaspoon salt
½ cup (1 stick) butter or
  margarine

¼ cup vegetable shortening
5 tablespoons cold water

1. In a medium-size bowl, combine the flour and salt. With a pastry blender or 2 knives, cut the butter and shortening into the flour mixture until the mixture resembles coarse crumbs.

2. Sprinkle the cold water over the flour mixture, 1 tablespoon at a time, and mix lightly until the pastry holds together when lightly pressed. Shape the pastry into 2 equal-size balls; flatten each half to a 1-inch thickness. Wrap and refrigerate the pastry at least 30 minutes.

FLUTING THE EDGE

Just before adding the top pastry to a two-crust pie, use a pastry brush to moisten the bottom pastry with a little water along the rim of the plate. Lay the top crust over the pie filling and gently press along the rim where the two pastries meet. Carefully fold the edge of the top crust under the edge of the bottom crust, making a soft rolled border that is even with the rim of the plate.

At this point you can flute the edge by pressing the pastry every inch or so to the rim with the tines of a fork, or you can make a more decorative scalloped edge that provides a higher pastry border for the pie. Gently pinch the border of dough with the thumb and forefinger of one hand while pressing it outward with the forefinger of the other hand. This scalloped edge is beautiful but also particularly good for an open-face fruit-filled pie that might tend to be juicy and bubble over.

Pastry for Tart or Tartlets

....

Pastry for a tart is generally sweeter, richer, and firmer than pie pastry and needn't be handled as carefully. It produces not a flaky crust but a delicate, short, and slightly crumbly one. Scraps can be rolled out, cut with a cookie cutter, and baked into snacks.

1 cup all-purpose flour	*⅓ cup butter or margarine*
1 tablespoon sugar	*1 egg, beaten*

1. In a medium-size bowl, combine the flour and sugar. With a pastry blender or 2 knives, cut the butter into the flour mixture until the mixture resembles coarse crumbs.

2. Add the egg to the flour mixture, and mix lightly just until the mixture holds together. If the pastry is too sticky, sprinkle lightly with more flour. Shape the pastry into a ball; flatten to a 1-inch thickness. Wrap and refrigerate the pastry at least 30 minutes.

Baked Tart Shell

Heat the oven to 400°F. On a lightly floured surface, roll out the pastry into an 11-inch round. Fit the pastry into a 9-inch fluted tart pan with a removable bottom. With a fork, pierce the bottom and side of the tart shell. Line the tart shell with aluminum foil and fill with uncooked dried beans or pie weights. Bake the pastry 15 minutes; remove the beans and foil and bake the tart shell 10 minutes, or until golden. Cool the tart shell completely on a wire rack before filling.

Graham-Cracker Crust

....

MAKES ONE 9-INCH CRACKER CRUST

⅓ cup butter or margarine   ¼ cup sugar
1½ cups graham-cracker
    crumbs

1. Heat the oven to 350°F. In a small saucepan, melt the butter over low heat. Remove from the heat, and stir in the crumbs and sugar until well mixed.

2. Press the crumb mixture into the bottom and side of a 9-inch pie plate, making a raised edge around the rim of the plate.

3. Bake the crust 8 minutes. Cool on a wire rack before filling.

THE OTHER COOKIE CRUSTS

Cookie-crumb crusts have been part of home bakers' repertoires for years and quite often are considered a staple to have on hand in the freezer. You might remember a grandmother or aunt saving broken cookies to be used for future cookie crusts. Some believe they were invented by frugal home bakers as a way to use leftover bread, crackers, and cookies.

To turn cookies and crackers into crumbs, process them in a blender or food processor until fine. Or crush them with a rolling pin in a plastic bag until fine. One and a half cups of crumbs combined with ⅓ cup butter or margarine and ¼ cup sugar will make a crust for any 9-inch pie plate. Treat your invented crusts just like unbaked or baked graham-cracker crusts, depending on the kind of pie you will be making. Gingersnaps, chocolate wafers, vanilla wafers, amaretto biscuits, sweet and savory biscotti, savory flatbreads — any crisp cookie or cracker can become a crust.

Equivalents Tables

....

INGREDIENTS EQUIVALENTS

Granulated sugar ----------1 pound ----------------------2 cups
Brown sugar ------------1 pound ----------------------2¼ cups
Confectioners' sugar -------1 pound ----------------------4 cups
Walnuts, chopped ---------4 ounces----------------------¾ cup
Almonds, whole ---------5⅓ ounces ----------------------1 cup
    Unblanched, slivered ----1 pound ----------------------3½ cups
Flour (unsifted) ---------2½ ounces----------------------½ cup
            3½ ounces ----------------------¾ cups
            5 ounces ----------------------1 cup
Butter -------------------½ ounce --------------1 tablespoon ⅛ stick)
            2 ounces--------------4 tablespoons (½ stick)
            4 ounces --------------8 tablespoons (1 stick)
Apples (3 medium) --------1 pound ----------------------3 cups, sliced
            1⅔ cups, cooked chopped
Peaches (4 medium)--------1 pound----------------------2½ cups, sliced
Small berries ---------------1 pint ----------------------2 cups
Strawberries---------------1 pint----------------------2½ cups, sliced

MEASURING EQUIVALENTS

3 teaspoons ----------------------1 tablespoon
1½ teaspoons ----------------------½ tablespoon
16 tablespoons ----------------------1 cup
8 tablespoons----------------------½ cup
1 liquid ounce ----------------------2 tablespoons
4 liquid ounces ----------------------½ cup
4 cups----------------------1 quart
2 cups ----------------------1 pint
4 quarts----------------------1 gallon
1 pound ----------------------16 ounces

Conversions Table

....

WEIGHTS

Ounces & Pounds	Metric Equivalents
¼ ounce	7 grams
⅓ ounce	10 grams
½ ounce	14 grams
1 ounce	28 grams
1¾ ounces	50 grams
2 ounces	57 grams
2⅔ ounces	75 grams
3 ounces	85 grams
3½ ounces	100 grams
4 ounces (¼ pound)	114 grams
6 ounces	170 grams
8 ounces (½ pound)	227 grams
9 ounces	250 grams
16 ounces (1 pound)	464 grams
1.1 pounds	500 grams
2.2 pounds	1,000 grams (1 kilogram)

TEMPERATURES

°F (Fahrenheit)	°C (Centigrade or Celsius)
32 (water freezes)	0
108-110 (warm)	42-43
140	60
203 (water simmers)	95
212 (water boils)	100
225 (very slow oven)	107.2
245	120
266	130
300 (slow oven)	149
350 (moderate oven)	177
375	191
400 (hot oven)	205
425	218
450	232
500 (very hot oven)	260

LIQUID MEASURES

tsp.: teaspoon
Tbs.: tablespoon
8 ounces = 1 cup

U.S. Spoons & Cups	Metric Equivalents	U.S. Spoons & Cups	Metric Equivalents
1 tsp.	5 milliliters	⅓ cup + 1 Tbs.	1 deciliter (100 milliliters)
2 tsp.	10 milliliters	1 cup	240 milliliters
3 tsp. (1 Tbs.)	15 milliliters	1 cup + 1¼ Tbs.	¼ liter
3⅓ Tbs.	½ deciliter (50 milliliters)	2 cups	480 milliliters
¼ cup	60 milliliters	2 cups + 2½ Tbs.	½ liter
⅓ cup	85 milliliters	4 cups	960 milliliters
		4⅓ cups	1 liter (1,000 milliliters)